Copyright © 1984 Concordia Publishing House
3558 S. Jefferson Avenue, St. Louis, MO 63118
Manufactured in the United States of America

Friedrich, Elizabeth, 1949—
    The Story of God's Love.

Summary: Brief retellings of selected Old and New Testament stories.
1. Bible stories, English. 1. (Bible stories)
I. Mitter, Kathy, ill. II. Title
BS551.2.F74 1985   220.9′505   85-7811
ISBN: 0-570-04122-8

    2   3   4   5   6   7   8   9   10   PP   94   93   92   91   90   89   88   87

Contents

When God Made the World

A long, long time ago there was no world.

There were no people or birds. There were no trees or flowers.

Only God was there.

Then God made EVERYTHING there is.

How did God do this?

He spoke—and it was so.

At first it was very dark, and water covered everything. So God said, "Let there be light." And there WAS light!

God divided the light from the dark and made night and day.

The next day God said, "Let there be a sky above."

As soon as God said it, there it was—a blue sky and fresh air high above the water.

On the third day God put all the water into ponds and lakes and clouds and rivers and oceans. He put land between the water.

Then God said, "Let plants grow on the dry land."

Right away bushes and berries, oak trees and orange trees grew. Green grass filled the fields. Tall trees grew little leaves. Red roses smelled so sweet.

On the fourth day God said, "Let lights shine in the sky."

Then sunshine warmed the world. The moon and stars shone at night.

The next day God worked again. He said, "Let fish fill the water. Let birds fill the air."

At once great whales and tiny fish swam in the waters. Crabs walked on the bottom of the sea.

Doves and ducks flew in the air. Owls sat high in the trees. Songs and sounds were all around.

On the sixth day God said, "Let animals walk on the land." And there they were!

Cows ate grass.

Mice ran in the fields.

Dogs and cats played.

Rabbits hopped.

Bears slept in caves.

Monkeys climbed trees.

Animals of all sizes lived in God's wonderful world.

Last of all God made a man and a woman.

God looked at the world. He had made such wonderful things. The biggest star was very good. The smallest ant was very good.

God was pleased with the world He made.

God said, "It is good. It is very, very good."

Genesis 1

5

Life in the Garden

God's world was beautiful.
Flowers grew on high hills.
Deer ran in the woods.
Bluebirds made soft nests.

Then God said, "Now I will
make a person."

God made Adam from the dust
of the earth.

God breathed into his nose—
and Adam became alive.

God wanted Adam to have
a good home. So God planted
a beautiful garden for him.
The garden was in a place
called Eden.

God put Adam into this garden.
He put Adam into the garden
of Eden.

The garden of Eden was
the most beautiful place
in God's whole world.

Fresh fruit hung from trees.
Berries and flowers grew
on the ground.

A river watered the garden.

God told Adam to live in the
garden and take care of it.

God said, "You may eat fruit
from all the trees—but not
from the tree in the middle
of the garden. If you eat from
that tree, you will die."

Then God asked Adam to give
each animal a name.

So, one by one, Adam named
all the animals.

He named the tiger and the
bee; the lion and the fly.

He named the cat, the dog,
the rat, the frog,
and all the rest.

Adam loved the garden.
He was close to God.
He had all the food he needed.
All the animals were kind.

But sometimes Adam was lonely.

Then God said, "It is not good
for the man to be alone. I will
make a helper for him. I will
give him a very special friend."

God made Adam fall into a
deep sleep.

Then God took one of Adam's
ribs. He made a woman out of the
rib. God brought her to Adam.

Adam was so glad. He said,
"At last I have someone like me."

He named the woman Eve.

Adam and Eve were husband
and wife. They loved each other
very much.

They took care of the garden.
They were never sick or sad.

God loved Adam and Eve.
He visited them often.

Adam and Eve were always glad
to see Him.

God was their best Friend!

Genesis 2

The First Sin

One day Eve was walking in the Garden of Eden.

She came close to the tree in the middle of the garden.

There she met the devil. He was hiding in a snake.

The snake said, "Listen, did God really tell you not to eat any of the fruit in the garden?"

Eve answered, "No. God did not say that. God said we may eat the fruit from all the trees but one. God told us not to eat from the tree in the middle of the garden. If we even touch that tree, we will die."

The snake said, "That is not true. You won't die. Listen! God knows that if you eat from this tree, you will be wise. You will be like God."

Eve looked at the tree again. The fruit was big and ripe. And Eve DID want to be like God.

So she took some fruit and ate it. She gave Adam some of the fruit, and he ate it too.

Adam and Eve did not obey God. This was the first sin.

Adam and Eve knew they had not obeyed God. They felt so ashamed that they hid in the bushes.

That evening God came to the garden. He found Adam and Eve right away.

God asked, "Adam, why are you hiding? Did you eat the fruit I told you not to eat?"

Adam said, "Well, the woman You gave me as a helper—she gave me the fruit."

Then God asked Eve, "What have you done?"

Eve answered, "The snake tricked me."

Adam blamed his wife. Eve blamed the snake. How sad!

Adam and Eve no longer trusted God. They did not say they were sorry. They were afraid and ashamed.

But God still loved them. God made warm clothes for them. He also gave them a wonderful promise.

God said to the devil, "One day I will send My Son to be born of a woman. He will have to suffer and die, but He will destroy your power. He will be the Savior of all people."

Adam and Eve had to leave the beautiful garden. They had to look for a new home.

Now they had to work hard to grow food. They could not just pick fruit from the trees anymore.

And sometimes they got tired. Sometimes they were hurt. Sometimes they cried. One day they would die.

But they never forgot God's wonderful promise. They believed God's promise would come true. They waited for the Savior.

Genesis 3

Cain and Abel

Adam and Eve found a new home. They worked hard just to grow food and keep warm.

One day God gave Adam and Eve a gift. He gave them a baby boy. They named him Cain.

Adam and Eve were very happy.

Later, God gave Adam and Eve another son. They named him Abel.

The boys grew fast.

They learned many things.

They learned to walk and talk. They learned how to plant seeds for food.

They learned how to take care of animals.

Adam and Eve told their sons about God.

Adam and Eve said to Cain and Abel, "God loves you very much. Someday He will send a Savior. We pray that you will always love and obey God."

Many years passed. Cain was a farmer. He liked to plant seeds and watch them grow.

Abel was a shepherd. He took care of his sheep and lambs. He helped them find the best grass to eat.

One day Cain and Abel brought gifts to God. Cain brought food he had grown. Abel brought his best little lamb.

Abel prayed and thanked God with all his heart. He loved God and tried to obey Him.

God was happy with his gift.

But Cain prayed and thanked God only with his words. He did not love or obey God.

God saw inside Cain's heart. God was not happy with Cain or his gift.

Cain was angry. He started to hate his brother.

One day Cain said to Abel, "Let's go to the field."

When they got to the field, Cain killed his brother.

God saw what Cain had done.

God asked Cain, "Where is your brother Abel?"

Cain answered, "I don't know. Do I have to take care of my brother?"

Then God said, "Why did you kill your brother? Now I must punish you. Your plants will not grow. You will not have a home. For the rest of your life you will walk from one place to another."

Cain said, "This is too hard. People will try to kill me."

So God put a mark on Cain. This mark told people not to kill Cain. God kept him safe.

Adam and Eve lost both sons. But God gave them another son. They named him Seth.

God also gave Adam and Eve many more children.

Genesis 4

The Flood

God's world began to fill with all kinds of people.

One was a man named Noah.

Noah and his family loved God. All the other people on earth were wicked. They did not love God at all.

God was angry with them.

One day God told Noah, "I will send a big flood. The wicked people will all drown. But I will keep you safe when the flood comes."

"Build an ark," God said. "I will keep you safe in an ark."

The ark was a big boat with a roof on it.

God told Noah, "Make the ark so big that you, your wife, your sons, and their wives can all live on it. Make room for animals and birds, too."

Noah did what God told him. He built a big ark. It was very long and very wide and very high. It had lots of rooms.

Noah made the ark out of wood. Then he covered it with tar.

When the ark was ready, God told Noah, "Put every kind of animal and bird in the ark. Take food to feed your family and all the animals."

Then Noah and his family climbed on.

All the animals came too. Lions, lizards, spiders, and sheep all climbed into the ark. Then God shut the door.

It rained and rained and rained some more.

Each day the water grew deeper. It rained every day and every night for 40 days and 40 nights.

The water hid the highest hills. But Noah's ark floated safely on top of the water.

At last it stopped raining. The winds blew and the sun shone. The water started to go away. When the ground was dry, everyone left the ark.

Noah, his family, and the animals stepped out onto dry ground.

God had kept Noah and his family safe and dry.

Noah was very happy. He built an altar to thank and praise God.

Then Noah looked up at the sky. He saw a beautiful rainbow. It was red, orange, yellow, green, blue, and purple.

God said, "I put the rainbow in the sky. I promise that I will never again send a flood to cover the world. Each time you see a rainbow, remember how much I love you."

Genesis 6—9

Abraham's Call

Noah's sons had many children and grandchildren and great-grandchildren.

Soon people lived all over the world again.

One of these people was Abraham.

Abraham lived in Haran.

One day God said to him, "I want you to leave your home. Leave your friends and follow Me. I will show you a new land. I want you to live there.

"Then I will give you a son. He will have many children and grandchildren.

"The whole land will be filled with your children.

"Someday the Savior will be born in your family."

Abraham believed God. He was not afraid to obey Him.

Abraham said, "I will go to the new land."

So Abraham said good-bye to all his friends. He went to the new land.

His wife, Sarah, went with him. Abraham also took his cows, sheep, and camels.

Servants came along to care for the animals.

Lot and his family went with Abraham. Abraham was Lot's uncle.

They went a long way.

Each night they slept in tents. Each morning they followed God to the new land.

Sometimes it was hot and dusty. Wolves howled, and winds blew.

But God took care of them.

God led Abraham to the new land. It was called Canaan.

At last they came to Caanan. Abraham saw rivers in green valleys. He saw trees filled with fruit.

God said, "This is the land I will give to your children."

Abraham built an altar. He thanked God for his new home.

Many years went by.

Abraham was very old.

But he still did not have any children.

God told Abraham, "I promise that I will give you a son. Count the stars in the sky. You will have that many children. You won't even be able to count them all. And I will be their God."

Abraham knew God would keep His promise.

He trusted God, and waited for his son to be born.

Abraham knew that someday his children's children would fill the land of Caanan.

Genesis 12—17

The Birth of Isaac

Abraham was almost 100 years old, but Sarah *still* did not have a son.

One day Abraham sat by his tent.

He looked up and saw three men walking toward him.

They were God and two angels.

Abraham ran to meet them.

Abraham bowed down and said, "Please stop at my home. You can rest under the trees. I will bring cool water to wash your feet. I will bring food for you to eat."

The men said, "Thank you. We will stay."

Abraham rushed into the tent. He said to Sarah, "We have company. Bake some bread for them. Hurry!"

Then Abraham got some meat, some butter, and some milk.

Abraham and Sarah prepared enough food for everyone.

Then Abraham served the three visitors.

The visitors asked Abraham, "Where is your wife Sarah?"

Abraham answered, "She is in the tent."

God said, "When I come again, Sarah will have a son."

Sarah was at the tent door. She was listening.

She laughed at God's words.

Sarah thought, "I'm too old to have a baby!"

God knew Sarah laughed.

He asked Abraham, "Why did Sarah laugh? Is anything too hard for God?"

Now Sarah became afraid.

She said, "I did not laugh."

But God said, "Yes, you did laugh."

Then the men left.

Later God gave Abraham and Sarah a baby boy. Oh, how happy they were!

Sarah said, "Now I will laugh because God has made me happy. And everybody will laugh with me."

Abraham and Sarah named their boy Isaac.

Isaac means "He laughs."

God had kept His promise. Abraham and Sarah knew that He would keep His other promises, too.

One day God would send His Son to be the Savior of the world.

Genesis 18—21

Jacob Tricks Esau

When Isaac grew up, he married Rebekah. They had twin sons, Esau and Jacob.

Isaac liked Esau better, but Rebekah loved Jacob more.

Esau liked the outdoors. His skin felt rough and hairy.

Jacob was a quiet boy. He liked to stay in his tent. His skin felt smooth and soft.

Isaac grew old and blind.

One day he said to Esau, "Son, I am old. I may die soon. Hunt an animal for me. Cook it the way I like it. I will eat it. Then I will bless you. When I die, you will be the head of the family."

Rebekah heard them talking. She did not want Isaac to bless Esau.

She wanted him to bless Jacob.

Esau went out to hunt. Then Rebekah found Jacob.

Rebekah said, "Isaac plans to bless Esau. You must do what I say. Get me two goats to cook. Take the food to your father. He will think you are Esau. He will bless you."

Jacob said, "If my father touches me, he will know I am not Esau."

His mother answered, "Just do what I say."

So Jacob got the goats, and Rebekah cooked them. Then she put Esau's clothes on Jacob. She also put goat hair on Jacob's neck and hands.

Jacob took the food to Isaac. Isaac asked, "Who are you?"

Jacob lied to his father.

Jacob said, "I am Esau. Please eat the meat. Then bless me."

Isaac said, "Come here. I want to touch you."

Isaac felt Jacob's hands and arms.

Isaac said, "You have Jacob's voice, but these are Esau's arms. Are you really Esau?"

Jacob answered, "I am."

Then Jacob kissed Isaac.

Isaac smelled the outdoors in Esau's clothes. He was sure it was Esau. Isaac blessed Jacob, and Jacob left.

Then Esau came in. He said, "I am here. Please eat the meat. Then give me your best blessing."

Isaac asked, "Who are you?"

Esau said, "I am Esau."

Isaac's whole body shook.

Isaac said, "I gave my blessing to Jacob. He tricked me. But the blessing is his forever. It cannot be changed."

Now Esau hated Jacob. He said to himself, "When my father dies, I will kill my brother Jacob."

Someone told Rebekah about Esau's plan.

Rebekah told Jacob, "Esau wants to kill you. Go stay with my brother Laban until it is safe to come home."

Genesis 27

Jacob's Ladder

It was a long trip to Uncle Laban's house.

The road was steep and stony. But Jacob walked quickly. He was afraid Esau would find him.

Jacob felt all alone. He missed his father and mother. He did not know if he would ever see them again.

The sun set. The sky grew dark.

Jacob stopped to rest for the night.

He did not have a tent to sleep in. He just lay down on the ground and rested his head on a stone.

Jacob fell asleep. He dreamed.

Jacob saw a ladder in his dream. One end of the ladder was on the ground. The other end went up, up, up into heaven.

Angels walked up and down the long ladder.

God stood at the very top.

God said, "I will give this land to you and your children. You will have many, many children and grandchildren.

"Someday I will send a Savior," God told Jacob. "He will be born in your family. Don't forget. I will always be with you. I will take care of you. I will bring you back to this land."

Then Jacob woke up.

He said, "God is close to me. I did not know it, but God is right here! What a wonderful place this is. This is the gate to heaven."

Jacob took the stone he had used as a pillow. He used the stone to mark that place. This was the place where God talked to him.

Jacob named the place *Bethel*. That word means "house of God."

Then Jacob prayed to God. Jacob said, "Thank You for staying with me. Thank You for taking care of me. You will always be my God. This stone will be Your house. I will give back to You part of all You give me."

Then Jacob went on his way. He still had to walk many miles. But he no longer felt alone. He knew God was with him. God was his Friend.

Genesis 28:10-22

Jacob's Return

Jacob lived and worked at his uncle Laban's house. He took care of the goats and sheep for many years.

Jacob married Laban's daughters.

First he married Leah.

Then he married Rachel.

God gave them many children.

Jacob worked hard. At last he had his own goats, sheep, camels, and other animals.

Jacob became a rich man.

One day God said to Jacob, "Go back to your own land. I will be with you."

Jacob got ready to go back to the land of Canaan.

His wives and children rode high on the backs of camels.

His sheep and goats walked ahead.

Laban did not want Jacob to leave.

But God told Laban, "Don't stop Jacob. Let him go."

Then Laban told Jacob, "May God watch over us the whole time we are apart."

Jacob went on his way. God sent angels to take care of him.

Soon Jacob would meet Esau.

Jacob was afraid of Easu. He sent some men to find out if Esau was still angry.

The men came back and said, "Esau is coming to meet you. He has 400 men with him."

Now Jacob was really afraid. He felt sure Esau wanted to kill him and his family.

Jacob prayed, "Please hear me, God! You told me to go back home. You said You would be with me. Please keep Your promise. Save me from Esau!"

The next day Jacob thought, "If I give gifts to Esau, maybe he will forgive me."

Jacob sent goats, sheep, camels, and cows to Esau.

God was with Jacob.

The next morning Jacob looked up. He saw Esau coming down the road.

Jacob bowed down seven times.

Esau ran to meet Jacob.

He threw his arms around Jacob and kissed him.

They both cried with joy.

Esau looked around. He saw Jacob's wives and children.

Esau asked, "Who are all these people?"

Jacob said, "These are the children God gave me. God is kind to me. He gives me all I need."

That same day Esau left.

Jacob went on to Canaan. At last he was home again.

Genesis 31—33

Joseph Is Sold

Jacob loved his son Joseph. Jacob gave Joseph a beautiful coat.

Joseph's brothers became jealous. They knew their father loved Joseph more than he loved them.

Joseph and his brothers took care of sheep and goats.

Sometimes Joseph's brothers did bad things. Then Joseph would run home to tell Jacob.

The brothers did not like this at all. They said mean things to Joseph.

One night Joseph had a dream.

He told his brothers, "Listen to my dream. We were at work in the field. My bundle of wheat stood up. All your bundles bowed down to mine."

Joseph's brothers asked, "Do you think you will be like a king, to rule over us?"

Joseph had another dream.

He told his brothers, "The sun, moon, and stars bowed down to me."

Now Joseph's brothers hated Joseph more than ever.

One day Jacob said to Joseph, "Go see if your brothers are safe. They are far away watching sheep."

Joseph put on his beautiful long coat and went to find his brothers.

Joseph's brother saw him coming. They said, "Here comes the dreamer. Let's kill him.

That will end his dreams."

Reuben, the oldest brother, tried to save Joseph. He said, "Let's not kill him. Just put him into this deep hole."

Reuben planned to go back later and take Joseph out of the hole.

So the brothers threw Joseph into the deep hole.

Then Reuben went away to look after the sheep.

A little later some men on camels came riding by. These men bought and sold things.

One brother said, "Let's sell Joseph to these men. That will be better than killing him."

So that is what they did.

Later Reuben came back to save Joseph. He looked into the hole and said, "Joseph is gone! Now what can we tell our father?"

The brothers said, "Let's kill a goat and put its blood on Joseph's coat. Our father will think an animal killed Joseph."

That is what they did.

Then they took the coat to their father Jacob. They said, "Look! We found this coat! Doesn't it belong to Joseph?"

Jacob looked at the coat. He said, "Yes, it is his coat! A wild animal has killed my son!"

Jacob was very sad. He cried and cried. He missed Joseph very much.

Genesis 37

25

Joseph Becomes a Ruler

Joseph went with the men who bought him.

They took him along to Egypt. There they sold him to a rich man. Joseph worked in the rich man's house.

Joseph did his work well.

But one day the rich man's wife became angry with Joseph. She told lies about him.

The rich man believed her lies. He put Joseph into prison.

God stayed with Joseph, even when he was in prison.

One night two men in prison had strange dreams. God made Joseph wise, and Joseph told them what their dreams meant.

Two years later the king of Egypt had two dreams.

The next morning he asked all his wise men to come to him.

The king asked them, "What do my dreams mean?"

No one could tell him.

The king's helper said, "I know someone who can tell you. I had a dream when I was in prison. A man named Joseph was in prison, too. He told me what the dream meant."

The king sent for Joseph.

The king told him, "I had two dreams last night. Can you tell me what they mean?"

Joseph answered, "God will help me tell you what they mean."

So the king told Joseph his dreams.

Then Joseph said, "Both dreams mean the same thing. There will be seven good years. A lot of food will grow. Then there will be seven bad years. Very little food will grow."

The king said, "Oh, no! Will we all die?"

Joseph told him, "No. But you must find a wise person to save food in the good years. When the bad years come, you can eat the food you saved."

The king liked Joseph's plan.

The king said, "You are the best person to do this job. God is with you. He has made you wise and good. You will help me rule over Egypt."

The king gave Joseph his ring. He also gave him many gifts.

The king said, "Everyone must obey Joseph, just as they obey me."

Joseph rode in the king's chariot.

Soldiers shouted, "Make way! Bow down!"

Joseph saved food in the seven good years. In every city he filled all the barns with food.

Then the seven bad years came. Hardly any food grew in the fields.

The people in Egypt were hungry. People all over the world were hungry. They came to Joseph in the land of Egypt to buy food.

Genesis 39—41

Joseph Forgives His Brothers

Joseph's family still lived in Canaan. They were hungry.

Father Jacob said to his sons, "Go to Egypt. Buy some food for us."

So the brothers went on their way—all of them except their little brother, Benjamin.

Benjamin stayed home with Jacob, his father.

The brothers came to Egypt. They bowed down to the ground in front of Joseph.

Joseph knew who they were, but they did not know him.

Joseph asked himself, "Are my brothers still wicked?"

He wanted to find out. So he said, "You are all spies."

Then Joseph put them into prison.

Now the brothers remembered their sin against Joseph.

They said to one another, "We did wrong to our brother."

Three days later Joseph told his brothers, "You may buy food and go home. But you must come back. Next time bring your brother Benjamin."

Joseph's brothers went home. When the food was gone, they came back. Benjamin came with them.

This time Joseph treated his brothers kindly. He invited them to his house for dinner.

After dinner, Joseph told a servant, "Fill the men's bags with food. Put my silver cup into Benjamin's bag."

Right after the brothers left, Joseph sent a servant after them.

The servant said, "Let me see your bags. You stole Joseph's cup."

Sure enough, the servant found the cup in Benjamin's bag.

So the brothers went back to see Joseph. They bowed before him again.

Joseph said, "Benjamin stole my cup. Now he must be my slave. The rest of you may go home."

One brother said, "We can't leave without Benjamin. I promised to take care of him. Our father has lost one son. He will die if he loses Benjamin. Let ME be your slave!"

Now Joseph was happy. His brothers loved Benjamin. And they loved their father.

Joseph said, "I am Joseph! I am your brother!"

Now the brothers were even more afraid. They thought, "We sold Joseph. Now he will punish us."

But Joseph did not punish them. Joseph said, "I forgive you."

Then he said, "Bring my father to Egypt. Bring your wives and children. Don't worry. God sent me here to keep many people alive."

Now Jacob was glad. His son Joseph was still alive!

Genesis 42—47

The Birth of Moses

Jacob and his children went to live in the land of Egypt.

Jacob's grandchildren and great-grandchildren grew up in the land of Egypt, too.

Their family grew very large. They filled many cities.

They called themselves the people of Israel.

The new king of Egypt began to worry about the people of Israel. He did not remember Joseph.

He said, "These people are too strong. There are too many of them. They might try to rule our land. We must make them weak."

So the king made the people of Israel his slaves. He made them work very, very hard.

But God took care of His people. He kept them strong.

Then the king said, "Throw all their boy babies into the river."

This made the people of Israel afraid and very sad. The mothers tried to hide their babies.

Aaron and Miriam had a baby brother. They helped their mother hide their baby brother.

At first they hid the baby in their house.

But soon the baby got too big. He cried too loudly. His mother could not hide him any more.

So the mother made a basket for her baby. She put him into it. Then she hid him in the tall grass by the river.

The basket floated like a little boat. Miriam hid near the river to watch the baby.

Soon the king's daughter, a princess, came to the river. She wanted to take a bath.

The princess saw the basket. She said to her servants, "Get that basket for me."

The princess opened the basket. She saw a beautiful baby boy. He was crying, and she felt sorry for him.

She said, "I want to keep this baby. He will be my son. I will name him Moses."

Miriam ran to the princess. She asked, "Do you need help? I know someone who can help. She can take care of the baby for you. Should I get her?"

The princess said, "Yes."

So Miriam got her mother.

The princess said, "Please take this baby. Feed him. Take care of him. Help him grow up. Then bring him to me. He will be my son."

Miriam and Aaron were happy. Moses' father and mother were very happy. Moses would live! God had taken care of him.

Exodus 1—2

The Burning Bush

Baby Moses grew and grew. His mother fed him. His mother took care of him. His mother told him about God.

Moses grew still bigger. Then he went to live in the palace with the princess.

She gave him the best food and toys. Moses went to school in the palace.

Moses lived in the palace until he was a man. Then he went far away. He lived in the desert.

One day, in this desert place, Moses saw a bush on fire. But the bush wasn't burning up! Its leaves were still green.

Then Moses heard a voice. The voice came from the bush.

The voice said, "Moses! Moses!"

Moses answered, "Here I am."

The voice said, "Don't come any closer. Take off your shoes. This is holy ground. I am God."

Then God said, "The people of Israel are praying to Me. I want to help them. I want to take them out of Egypt. I want to take them back to Canaan. You will lead them."

Moses said, "Who am I? How can I do that?"

God said, "I will be with you. Tell them the Lord picked you to lead them."

Moses asked, "What if they don't believe me?"

God said "What is in your hand?"

Moses answered, "A walking stick."

God said, "Throw the stick on the ground."

Moses threw the stick down. God turned it into a snake.

God said to Moses, "Pick it up by the tail."

Moses picked up the snake. It became a walking stick again!

God said, "Show this to the people of Israel. Then they will know I have sent you."

Then Moses said, "I can't speak well."

God said, "I will help you speak. I will tell you what to say."

Moses did not want to go. He said, "Please send someone else."

God answered, "Your brother Aaron can speak well. I will send him with you. He will help you."

Then Moses left the desert. God sent Aaron to meet him.

Aaron talked to the people of Israel. He told them, "God will save you. He will take you out of Egypt. He will take you back to Canaan."

Then Moses threw down his stick. It turned into a snake. Then it turned back into a stick.

The people of Israel believed Aaron and Moses. They believed God. Now they were happy.

Exodus 3—4

Moses and
the King

God sent Moses and Aaron to see the king.

They said, "God wants you to let His people go home."

The king wanted to keep the people of Israel in Egypt. He wanted them to work hard for him.

The king said, "I won't obey your God! I won't let the people go!"

Then the king made the people work even harder.

God told Moses, "The king will let My people go. I will send all kinds of trouble to Egypt. Then the king will let you go."

First all the water in Egypt turned to blood.

Then frogs jumped all over everything. Beds, bowls, and ovens were filled with frogs.

The king said to Moses, "Ask your God to take away the frogs. Then I will let your people go."

Moses prayed to God, and the frogs left.

As soon as the frogs were gone, the king changed his mind.

The king said, "I won't obey your God! I won't let the people go!"

More troubles came to Egypt. God sent lice and flies. God let the farm animals die. God sent boils, hail, and grasshoppers. He made days and nights very dark. But the king still would not obey God.

God said, "I will send one more trouble. Then the king will beg you to leave Egypt. Tell My people to kill a lamb. Tell them to put the lamb's blood on their doors. Tell them to get ready to leave the land of Egypt."

That night an angel came. The angel killed the oldest son in every home in Egypt. Even the king's son was killed.

But the angel *passed over* the homes with blood on the door. The people of Israel were safe.

The king sent for Moses.

The king said, "Get out! Leave my country! Take your people and go!"

The people of Israel left Egypt right away. A long line of men, women, children, and animals left Egypt. They started walking to the land of Canaan.

God led them in a cloud. At night he led them with fire.

Moses told the people, "Don't forget this day. Today God's angel *passed over* our homes. Today God set us free!"

Exodus 5—13

Crossing the Red Sea

The people of Israel camped by the Red Sea. They rested there. Then they would go on to Canaan.

But they did not rest very long. The king of Egypt had changed his mind again.

He said, "Why did I let those people go? We need them to work for us. We must bring them back."

The king told his soldiers. "Take your horses and chariots! Catch those people! Bring them back!"

The people of Israel saw the king and his army.

The people were afraid. The sea was in front of them. High mountains were on both sides. The soldiers were behind them.

The people asked Moses, "Why did you bring us here? The soldiers will kill us."

Moses answered, "Don't be afraid. God will save you today. You won't see the soldiers again."

Then God told Moses, "Lift your walking stick and hold it over the sea."

Moses did what God told him to do.

Then God sent a big wind. It pushed the water back. It made the sea floor dry.

The people of Israel walked on the sea floor. High walls of water rose on both sides of them.

The king and his army followed the people. They drove their horses and chariots onto the sea floor.

Then God stopped the army. The chariots slowed down. They could hardly move in the sand.

The soldiers said, "God is fighting for His people. Let's get out of here!"

But it was too late.

The people of Israel reached the other side, and God told Moses, "Hold your hand over the sea."

As soon as Moses did this, the water came back. The dry path was gone.

Water covered the king and his men. They all died. God's people were saved!

The people of Israel saw what God had done. They believed in Him. They all praised God. The women played music and danced.

Moses and all the people sang. They sang this song:

> I will sing to the Lord.
> He has saved His people.
> He has thrown the horses
>   and riders into the sea.
> I will praise the Lord
>   forever.

Exodus 14—15

Life in the
Wilderness

Moses led the people of Israel into the desert. The people saw sand and stones all around them. They did not see trees and grass. They did not find food to eat.

The sun shone hotter and hotter. The people of Israel were sad.

They asked one another, "Why did we leave Egypt? At least we could eat there. We had all the food we needed. We will die here in this desert. We will starve to death."

God said to Moses, "My people are crying for help. I have heard them. I will send food. It will be like rain from the sky. At night I will send meat. In the morning I will send bread."

Moses told the people, "God will give you food."

That night God sent quail. The people caught the birds. They cooked them for supper.

The next morning the people looked at the ground. Something was on the ground. The ground was as white as snow.

The people asked, "What is that? What is on the ground?"

Moses said, "This is bread. It is bread from God. Take as much as you need. But take only what you need today. God will send more food tomorrow."

The people of Israel called the food *manna*. It tasted like a honey cake.

On the sixth day Moses said, "Today take twice as much manna. God wants you to rest tomorrow. No manna will fall from the sky."

The people of Israel walked all over the desert. They ate the food God gave them.

One night the people set up their tents in the hills. Rocks were all around. There was no water to drink.

The people began to grumble again.

They said to Moses, "Why did you lead us out of Egypt? At least we had water there. Here we will die from thirst. Give us water to drink."

Moses prayed to God, "What can I do?"

God told him, "Hit that rock with your stick. Water will come out of it."

Moses hit the rock. Cool water came out of it. The people drank the water. They drank all they wanted.

God stayed with His people. He took care of them.

Exodus 16—17

The Giving of the Law

The people of Israel came to a high mountain. It was called Mount Sinai.

Moses went up the mountain. There he talked with God. The people waited down below.

God told Moses, "I love the people of Israel. I want them to always be My people. Tell them to get ready. In three days I will talk to them."

Moses went down the mountain. He told the people, "Get ready to worship God."

Everyone came to the mountain. The people heard loud thunder. They saw smoke and fire on the top of the mountain. They felt the mountain shake.

God began to speak. He told the people His holy laws, the *Ten Commandments*. God told the people, "Love Me. Love one another."

The people were afraid of the smoke, fire, and loud thunder. They moved back from the mountain.

Moses said, "Do not be afraid." Then Moses climbed back up Mount Sinai. He talked with God again.

God wrote His Ten Commandments on two large, flat pieces of stone. He gave the stones to Moses.

Moses stayed on the mountain 40 days and 40 nights.

The people grew tired of waiting.

They said to Aaron, "Maybe Moses will not come back. Make a god to lead us."

Aaron said, "Give me your gold earrings." Aaron took the earrings and made a golden calf from them.

The people said, "This is our god. We will pray to the golden calf."

God saw what His people were doing.

He said to Moses, "My people made a golden calf. They say the calf is their god. I am very angry. I want to kill them all."

Moses said, "Please don't kill Your people."

God heard Moses' prayer. He did not kill the people.

Moses went down from the mountain. He saw the people dancing around the golden calf.

Now Moses became angry. He broke the stones with the commandments from God.

Moses threw the golden calf into a fire and melted it. He punished all the people who did not love God.

Then Moses took two new pieces of stone up the mountain.

God wrote the Ten Commandments on these pieces of stone, and Moses taught them to the people.

Exodus 19—34

Building the Tabernacle

God wanted His people to love Him. He wanted them to love each other. Then they would always be happy.

God also wanted His people to remember His love for them.

So God said to Moses, "Tell the people to make a worship tent. It will be their church. Call it the tabernacle."

Then God said, "Use the tabernacle for offerings and prayer. Take it with you in the desert. Take it along to Canaan. It will remind you of My love. It will help you show love to Me."

God told Moses, "Make the tabernacle beautiful. Make the tent out of blue, purple, and red cloth. Sew pictures all over the cloth."

Then God said, "Put a box inside the tent. Take the two stones with the Ten Commandments. Put them into the box. Also put tables, lamps, oil, and an altar inside the tent. Cover everything with gold. Call the box the *Ark of the Covenant.*"

Moses said to the people, "We will build the tabernacle. Bring your gifts to God. Give them to me. I will use them to make the tabernacle."

So the people brought gifts. They brought gold rings and jewels. They brought fine cloth, leather, and silver. They brought colored thread, spices, and oil.

Moses took their gifts. He started to build the tabernacle. God chose two men to do the hardest work. God showed them how to make everything beautiful.

Each morning the people of Israel brought more gifts. The gifts showed their love for God.

Soon the builders said, "The people have brought many more gifts than we need."

So Moses told the people, "Stop bringing gifts. The builders have too much."

At last the tabernacle was done. Now God didn't call Moses to Mount Sinai any more. He talked to Moses right in the tabernacle.

A cloud covered the tabernacle. The bright light of God filled it.

Sometimes the cloud lifted from the tabernacle. Then the people would move their camp.

Sometimes the cloud covered the tabernacle. Then the people would not move their camp.

The people walked on to Canaan. God stayed with them.

All day they could see God's cloud. And all night God's fire burned in the sky over the tabernacle.

The people knew God was with them. They knew He loved them.

Exodus 35—40

Joshua Becomes Leader

The people of Israel walked on and on in the desert.

God always took care of them. But sometimes they were not happy.

One time the people said, "Moses, we hate this place. We don't have any figs or grapes to eat. We don't even have any water!"

Moses felt angry and tired. He went into the tabernacle. He prayed to God.

God said to Moses, "Speak to that rock over there. Water will come out of it."

Moses yelled at the people, "Do I have to get water out of this rock for you?" Moses hit the rock two times with his stick. Water came out of the rock.

But God was not happy. He said to Moses, "I told you to speak to the rock. But you hit it with your stick. You did not trust My power. Now you will not get to enter the land of Canaan."

The people of Israel walked in the desert for many years. At last they came close to the land of Canaan.

God said to Moses, "Climb up that mountain. I will show you the land. Then I will take you to heaven."

Moses said, "God, choose someone to lead your people."

God said, "I choose Joshua."

Moses put his hands on Joshua's head.

Moses told the people, "I will die soon. Then Joshua will be your leader."

Then Moses climbed to the top of the mountain. God showed him the whole land.

Moses saw palm trees and rivers. He saw fields, hills, and lakes. Then Moses died.

God told Joshua, "Moses is dead. Now you must lead My people. I will always be with you. Be strong. Listen to My Word. Obey My Commandments."

God said, "Cross the Jordan River. Go into the land of Canaan."

Joshua told the people, "Cook food and get ready. We will cross the Jordan River. We will go into Canaan."

The people came to the river. Some priests stepped into it. God stopped the water.

God made a big wall of water on one side. The water flowed away on the other side. The people walked across on dry ground.

God's people were safely home. God had kept His promise. He had led them back to Canaan, the Promised Land.

Numbers 20
Deuteronomy 31—34
Joshua 1—3

The Battle of Jericho

The people of Israel had come to Canaan.

They were out of the desert.

They were across the Jordan River.

They were home!

But wicked people lived in Canaan. They prayed to idols. They did not obey God.

These wicked people were afraid of the people of Israel. They knew God helped His people.

Many of the wicked people lived in the city of Jericho. This city had high, thick walls all around it.

One day the people of Israel came close to Jericho.

The people of Jericho saw them coming. They locked the strong city gate. Guards sat on top of the walls. They were ready to fight.

God told Joshua, "I want you and your soldiers to march around Jericho. March around the city once a day for six days. On the seventh day, march around the city seven times. Then blow the trumpets and tell the soldiers to shout. The city walls will fall down."

Joshua told his men to start marching. That day they marched around the city once.

On the second day they marched around the city once.

On the third day they marched around the city once.

On the fourth day they marched around the city once.

On the fifth day they marched around the city once.

On the sixth day they marched around the city once.

The people of Jericho must have thought, "What's going on? What are the people of Israel doing? Aren't they going to fight?"

On the seventh day, Joshua and his men got up early. They marched around the city seven times.

Then Joshua gave the signal. The men blew their trumpets. The soldiers shouted. And the walls of Jericho fell down flat.

The army of Israel ran into the city. They killed all the wicked people.

Then the people of Israel went on into the rest of the land of Canaan.

God gave them all they needed. They had homes to live in. They had sheep, milk, and honey.

Now the people were happy. They said, "We love God, and we will serve Him always. He brought us out of Egypt. He brought us to this beautiful land. He kept us safe the whole way. He is our God."

Joshua 6

47

Gideon

The people of Israel promised to love and serve God always.

But they soon forgot their promise. They did not obey God. They worshiped false gods.

Then God let robbers come into the land. The robbers stole grain, sheep, cows, and donkeys. The people of Israel hid from the robbers. They hid in caves.

One day a man came to Canaan. He sat under an oak tree and talked to Gideon.

Gideon did not know it, but the man was God Himself.

The man said to Gideon, "God is with you, brave man."

Gideon answered, "God has left our people. Now robbers are taking all our food and animals."

Then God said, "I am the Lord. I want you to chase the robbers away."

Gideon said, "I can't. I am not strong."

God told him, "I will help you."

Later on Gideon and his army went to chase the robbers away.

But God told Gideon, "You have too many soldiers. You must not trust in your army. You must not trust in yourself. You must trust Me. I said I will help you."

Then God said, "You need only a few men. Send the others back home."

Gideon obeyed God. He sent many men home. Finally, there were only 300 men left.

That night Gideon told his men, "Get up! God will help us chase the robbers away."

Gideon gave each man a trumpet. He also gave them a jar with a burning torch inside.

Gideon told the men, "Watch me. Do what I do."

Gideon and his men went all around the robber's camp.

Gideon blew his trumpet. He broke his jar. He held the burning torch high in the air. All his men did the same.

They all shouted, "A sword for the Lord and for Gideon!"

The robbers were afraid. They saw fire around their camp and heard so much noise. Gideon and his men chased the robbers out of the land.

The people of Israel were very happy. They said, "Gideon, please be our king. You saved us from the robbers."

But Gideon told them, "God is your King. He is the One who saved you."

Judges 6—7

Ruth

One year it was very dry in Canaan. Little food grew that year. Many people were hungry.

Naomi and her husband and their two sons left their home in Canaan. They went to find food in Moab.

Naomi's husband died in that faraway land. Her sons married Orpah and Ruth, two girls who lived in Moab.

About ten years later Naomi's sons died. Naomi felt very sad. She thought God had left her.

But one day Naomi heard good news. Food was growing in the land of Canaan again. Naomi wanted to go back home. She got ready to leave Moab.

Naomi told Orpah and Ruth, "Stay here. This is your home."

Naomi kissed the girls good-bye, and they started to cry.

Orpah said she would stay in Moab.

But Ruth said to Naomi, "Where you go, I will go. Where you live, I will live. Your people shall be my people, and your God shall be my God."

Then Ruth and Naomi walked to Canaan.

They were poor and all alone. One day Ruth said to Naomi, "We need food. I am going to pick up grain in the fields."

So Ruth went to the fields of a rich man named Boaz.

Boaz saw Ruth. He asked his workers, "Who is that girl?"

The workers answered, "Her name is Ruth. She came with Naomi from Moab. She has been kind to Naomi."

Boaz walked over to Ruth.

Boaz told Ruth, "You may always pick up grain in my fields. You are safe here."

Ruth asked Boaz, "Why are you so good to me?"

He said, "Because you are kind to Naomi."

Boaz gave Ruth water to drink and bread to eat.

Then Boaz told his workers, "Drop more grain in the field. Let Ruth pick it up."

Ruth worked all day. She took the grain home to Naomi.

Naomi saw all the grain.

She asked Ruth, "Where did you get this food?"

Ruth answered, "In the fields of a man named Boaz. He told me I could pick up as much as I wanted."

Naomi said, "May God bless Boaz! God is still taking care of us."

Later, Boaz and Ruth got married. God blessed them with a son. Their son was the grandfather of King David.

Many years later, Jesus was born from David's family.

The Book of Ruth

Samuel as a Boy

Hannah sat all alone by the tabernacle. She was crying.

Hannah wanted a baby. She had wanted a baby for a long time. But still she had no children.

Hannah prayed, "Dear God, please give me a son. If you do, I will will give him to You. He will serve You all his life."

At last God gave Hannah a son. She named him Samuel.

A few years later, Hannah dressed Samuel in a robe. She took him to the tabernacle.

Eli, the priest, was sitting at the door.

Hannah said, "I asked God for this child. God gave him to me. Now I am bringing my son to God. He will serve God all his life."

Samuel stayed with Eli. He helped Eli. Samuel loved and obeyed God.

Eli had two sons. Eli did not punish them when they did wrong things. When they grew up, they would not listen to Eli.

Now Eli was old and almost blind. Samuel stayed with him and helped him.

One night Samuel was sleeping. All at once he woke up. He heard someone calling him.

Samuel ran to Eli and said, "Here I am. You called me."

But Eli said, "Go to bed. I did not call you."

So Samuel went back to bed. Then he heard someone call him again, "Samuel! Samuel!"

Samuel got up and went to Eli. He said, "Here I am. You called me."

Again Eli told him, "Go to bed. I did not call you."

Samuel went back to bed again. Then he heard someone call him a third time.

Samuel got up and said, "Here I am, Eli. You called me."

Now Eli understood. God was calling Samuel. Eli told Samuel, "If you hear your name again, say, 'Speak, Lord, I am listening.'"

Samuel went back to bed. He heard God call, "Samuel! Samuel!"

Samuel answered, "Speak, Lord, I am listening."

Then God said, "Eli and his sons are going to die. The sons did wicked things, and Eli did not stop them."

The next morning Eli asked, "Samuel, what did God tell you?"

Samuel told him.

Eli said, "God will do what is best."

Soon after this there was a war. Eli's sons were killed. Eli died too.

God's words came true.

Now Samuel became God's priest and servant. When Samuel spoke, God was telling His people something special.

1 Samuel 1—4

Samuel Anoints David

One day the people of Israel told Samuel, "We want a king."

God told Samuel, "I choose Saul to be the king. He will be the first king of Israel.

"Pour olive oil on his head. This will show that I picked him."

Saul was king for many years. At first he was a good king. But later he did not obey God.

One day God told Samuel, "I have picked a new king. Get some olive oil and go to Bethlehem.

"Find a man called Jesse. I have chosen one of his sons. He will be the next king."

So Samuel did what God asked.

Then Jesse brought his oldest son to Samuel. This son was strong, tall, and good-looking.

Samuel thought, "He looks like he would be a good king. This must be the person God has picked."

But God said to Samuel, "This is not My chosen king. He looks good on the outside. But I look on the heart."

So Samuel told Jesse, "No, God has not chosen him."

Jesse brought another son.

Again Samuel said, "No, God has not chosen him."

One by one Jesse brought his sons to Samuel.

Each time Samuel said, "No, God has not chosen him."

At last Samuel asked Jesse, "Do you have any more sons?"

Jesse said, "I have one more son."

Samuel said, "Bring him to me."

Jesse sent for David.

David was Jesse's youngest son. He was in the fields, taking care of his sheep.

David came into the room. Samuel saw his pink cheeks and bright eyes.

Then God told Samuel, "This is the one I have chosen. He loves Me with all his heart. David will be the next king of Israel."

Samuel took some olive oil and poured a little on David's head. This meant David would be king after Saul died.

This was a special day. Now David knew he would be the next king.

God stayed with David and led him.

1 Samuel 16:1-13

David and Goliath

Saul and his soldiers were at war with the Philistines.

The Philistine army was strong. They had many soldiers.

One of them was a giant named Goliath. Goliath stood nine feet tall. He carried a huge sword and wore a heavy coat of iron.

Goliath made fun of the people of Israel and their God.

Every day Goliath shouted, "Send a man to fight me. If he kills me, we will be your slaves. If I kill him, you will be our slaves."

Saul and his army felt afraid. Goliath was so big and so strong! No one wanted to fight him.

Three of David's brothers fought in Saul's army.

But David stayed home to care for his father's sheep.

One day Jesse told David, "Find out how your brothers are. Take this food to them."

David took the food and went to find his brothers.

Just as David reached the army, Goliath came out to shout at the people of Israel.

David heard Goliath. Goliath made fun of God and His people.

David said, "I will fight Goliath."

Saul asked, "How can you fight a giant? You aren't even a soldier."

But David answered, "God will help me."

So Saul gave David a coat of iron and a big sword.

But David said, "I can't fight with all this." And he took it off.

David picked up his sling. He chose five smooth stones from the stream. Then he walked out to meet Goliath.

Goliath came closer and closer and still closer. He laughed when he saw David.

Goliath said, "Who are you? Where is your sword?

"Do you think I am a dog? Are you going to chase me away with your stick?"

David answered, "I don't need a sword to beat you. God is on my side."

David put one stone in his sling. He swung it over his head—faster and faster.

Then David let the stone fly at Goliath. It hit the giant in the head and killed him.

The Philistines saw that Goliath was dead. They started to run. Saul's army chased them far away.

1 Samuel 17

David and Saul

David became a leader in King Saul's army.

David lived at the palace with Saul and his son Jonathan. Jonathan and David were good friends.

God was with David. He always helped David's army.

One day people danced and sang in the streets. David was coming back after a big war.

The women sang, "King Saul has beaten thousands of enemies, but David has beaten TENS of thousands."

Saul did not like this song. He became jealous.

Saul said, "The people think David is better than me. Soon they will make him king."

Saul often became very angry. Sometimes he yelled and stamped his feet.

Still, David stayed at Saul's house. David would play his harp to help Saul feel better.

But Saul became angry with David again and again. Many times Saul tried to kill David.

At last David knew he must hide far away.

One morning David met Jonathan in the fields. The two friends said good-bye. Tears ran down their faces as they hugged each other. They knew they might never see each other again.

Then Jonathan said, "God be with you, my friend." And the two parted.

David hid in deserts, woods, and hills. He knew God was always with him.

Saul hunted all over the land for David.

One day David hid in a cave. Saul came into the cave to rest. He did not see David.

Some men with David said, "This is your chance! Sneak up quietly and kill Saul!"

Then David quietly went over to Saul. He cut off a corner of Saul's coat. Saul did not see or hear him.

A little later Saul left the cave. David ran after him.

David bowed down and said, "Look, I cut off a piece of your coat. I could have killed you, but I don't want to hurt you."

Tears came into Saul's eyes.

He told David, "I tried to kill you.

"But you have been good to me. You were kind to me, your enemy.

"May the Lord bless you. I'm sure God will make you king."

Then Saul went back home.

1 Samuel 18—24

Building the Temple

Saul ruled Israel for 40 years.

After he died, David became the king. David also ruled the country for 40 years.

David wanted to build a house of worship for God. It would be called a *temple*.

But God told David, "One of your sons will be the next king. I want HIM to build My temple."

David's son Solomon became the next king. God made Solomon very wise.

Solomon began to build a temple for God. He used the best stone and wood.

The workers cut all the stones very carefully.

They carved pictures of angels and flowers on the walls.

Then they covered all the pictures and walls with gold.

They covered the temple altar and the floor with gold.

They made the whole temple very beautiful.

God told Solomon to build a special room—called the *Most Holy Place*—in the temple.

The workers put the *ark of the covenant* in the Most Holy Place. This was the special box the people of Israel carried along in the desert after they left Egypt.

God had told the people to put some important things into the ark of the covenant. They put some manna into this box. They put Aaron's rod into the box.

And they put the pieces of stone with the Ten Commandments into the box.

Finally the temple was finished. Thousands of people had helped build the temple. It took them seven years to build it.

When it was finished, Solomon told the people, "Come and pray at the temple."

The priests brought the ark of the covenant to the temple. They carried the box into the Most Holy Place. At once God's shining light filled the temple.

Solomon prayed to God. Solomon said, "God, You are wonderful! You keep all Your promises.

"Now watch over this temple. Hear my prayers. Hear the prayers of all Your people.

"Hear us when there is no rain or food. Hear us when enemies attack us. Hear us when we are sick or sad.

"When we sin, forgive us, Lord. Then bring us back to You.

"Bless Your people, Lord. May they obey and love You today and always."

Solomon and the people stayed at the temple for seven days. Then they stayed another seven days. They praised God for all the blessings He had given them.

1 Kings 6 and 8

Elijah and the Prophets of Baal

Many years after Solomon died, Ahab became the king of Israel.

Ahab was a bad king. He prayed to Baal. Baal was a false god.

Many other people in Israel also prayed to Baal. They forgot the true God.

One day God sent Elijah to Ahab. Elijah told Ahab, "You pray to Baal. You make God angry. Now He will not send rain to Israel."

It did not rain in Israel for three years. The people had little food.

Ahab became angry. He tried to kill Elijah.

But God took care of Elijah. God gave him food, water, and a safe place to stay.

One day God said to Elijah, "I will send rain again. Go find King Ahab."

Elijah found Ahab. Elijah said, "Tell the people of Israel to meet me on Mount Carmel. Tell the priests of Baal to come, too."

The wicked king did this. His priests and the people came to Mount Carmel.

Elijah told the people, "You must make up your minds! Will you love God or Baal?

"Today we will find out which one is the true God.

"The priests of Baal will bring an offering to their god. I will bring an offering for the Lord.

"We will lay our offerings on altars. Then we will pray for fire. The god who sends fire will be the true God."

The people shouted, "That's a good test!"

The priests of the idol Baal had the first chance. They prayed and shouted all morning and afternoon. But there was no answer. No fire came.

Then Elijah set up stones for an altar. He dug a ditch all around it. He told some men to pour water over the altar and the wood and the offering. Water even filled the ditch around the altar.

Then Elijah prayed, "O Lord, show these people You are the one true God."

At once God sent fire down. The fire burned up the offering. It burned up the wood.

It even burned up the stones and dried up all the water in the ditch around the altar.

The people saw this. Then they shouted, "The Lord is God! The Lord is God!"

Soon dark clouds came to the sky. The wind blew. Great drops of rain began to fall.

The true God had sent fire. Now He was again sending rain to the land of Israel.

1 Kings 17—18

Elijah Goes to Heaven

Elisha walked down the road with his teacher, Elijah.

Elijah was going to visit friends in two nearby cities.

Elijah and Elisha came to the first city.

Elijah said, "Stay here, Elisha. I will go on alone."

But Elisha answered, "I am going with you. I won't leave you alone."

Elijah and Elisha came to the second city.

Elijah said, "Stay here, Elisha. I will go on alone."

Elisha answered again, "I am going with you. I won't leave you alone."

Some people of God lived in the cities. They came to Elisha. They told him, "God will take your teacher to heaven today."

Elisha answered, "Yes, I know."

At last Elijah and Elisha came to the Jordan River.

Elijah took off his coat. He hit the water with it. The water moved apart. Elijah and Elisha walked across on dry ground.

Then Elijah asked, "What do you want me to give you before God takes me to heaven?"

Elisha answered, "I want to be God's helper, like you are.

"I want God to bless me even more than He blessed you."

Elijah told him, "Look for a sign from God. Maybe you will see me when God takes me to heaven.

"This will be your sign. Then you will know that God has answered your prayer."

The two men walked and talked. All at once a wagon of fire came between them. Horses of fire pulled the wagon. Elijah went up to heaven in a whirlwind.

Elisha saw all this happen. He called, "My teacher, my teacher!" But Elijah was gone.

Elisha would not see his friend on earth anymore. He knew that. Now it was up to him to be God's prophet.

Elisha picked up Elijah's coat, which had fallen on the ground. He went back to the river. He hit the water with the coat.

Elisha shouted, "Where are You, Lord? Where is the God of Elijah?"

The water went apart, just as it had for Elijah. Now Elisha knew God would also bless him and help him.

2 Kings 2:1-15

Isaiah's Call

When Isaiah lived, many of God's people were rich.

They began to trust in the good things they had.

They did not help the poor people around them.

They even forgot about God.

So God chose Isaiah to warn them. He showed Himself to Isaiah in a special way.

Isaiah saw God sit on a throne. God's long robe filled the whole temple. All around God's throne there were many angels.

Each angel had six wings. With two wings they hid their faces. With two wings they covered their feet. And with two wings they flew.

The angels sang loudly, "Holy, holy, holy! The Lord God is holy! His glory fills the earth."

The angels' song shook the whole temple. And the temple was filled with smoke.

Isaiah said, "I have seen God with my own eyes. I know God is my King. He rules over the whole world."

Then Isaiah asked, "What can I do? I love God. But I am weak and sinful. And I live in a land of sinful people."

Then an angel flew down to Isaiah. The angel carried a burning coal from the altar in the temple. He touched Isaiah's lips with the coal.

The angel said, "Now your sin is taken away."

Isaiah knew God forgave His sins. He was a new person. He was ready to serve God.

Then God asked, "Whom shall I send? Who will speak to My people?"

Isaiah answered, "I will go! Send me!"

God said, "Go. Tell the people about their sin.

"Also tell them that I will send a Savior. He will take away their sin."

Isaiah did this. He told the people, "God will save you. A Child will be born. He will be your King. He will be wonderful. He will be called the Prince of peace."

Another time Isaiah said, "Many people will hate the Savior. They will hurt Him. They will kill Him. But because of His death we will be saved. The Lord is coming to save you!"

Isaiah 6, 9, and 53

When God Healed Hezekiah

God's people had many wicked kings. These kings did not obey God. They prayed to false gods.

Some wicked kings even locked the doors of the temple. Now no one could go inside to pray to God.

Then God let enemies come into the land. The enemies killed the people and stole from them.

At last Hezekiah became the king. Hezekiah was a good king. He loved and obeyed God. He chased the enemies away.

Hezekiah broke the statues of the false gods to pieces. He opened the temple doors. He brought offerings to God.

One day Hezekiah got sick. Isaiah came to see Hezekiah. Isaiah said, "Get ready to die, Hezekiah. You will not get well again."

Hezekiah felt sad when he heard this. He was still a young man.

Hezekiah wanted to do more things for God. He did not want to die yet.

So he turned his face to the wall and prayed to God.

Hezekiah prayed, "Lord, I have tried to do all the things You wanted. Remember how I have served You. Please let me live longer."

Then Hezekiah started to cry. God heard Hezekiah's prayer. Isaiah was just leaving the king's house. But God told him to go back to the king.

God told him to give Hezekiah a new message.

Isaiah told Hezekiah, "God has heard your prayer. He has seen your tears. He will make you well again. He will also help you chase the enemies away."

These promises from God made Hezekiah happy. He asked Isaiah, "What sign will God give me? How can I be sure God will make me well again?"

Isaiah said, "The sun's shadow will be your sign from God. Watch how it moves on the special stairs your father built. Shall the sun's shadow on the stairs move forward ten steps or back ten steps?"

Hezekiah answered, "When the sun goes forward, the shadow gets longer. It would be easy to make the shadow longer. Make it get shorter. Have it go back ten steps."

Isaiah prayed to God.

Then God made the shadow move back ten steps.

Three days later King Hezekiah was well again. He went to the temple to thank and praise God.

Hezekiah said, "I was going to die. I was weak and in pain. But now I will live. Play the harps! Sing praise to God! I will live for God alone."

2 Kings 20
Isaiah 38

Three Men in a Furnace

Shadrach, Meshach, and Abednego were far from their home.

Soldiers from Babylon had come to Jerusalem. The soldiers captured Shadrach, Meshach, and Abednego. They took them back to Babylon.

The three men had to work for the king of this faraway land.

One day the king told his workers to make a big statue out of gold.

The workers made the statue. Then the king called all his people together.

One of the king's men yelled, "Listen, people of all lands! This is the king's god. When you hear music, you must pray to this god. If you refuse, you will be put into a hot burning furnace."

Then the music played. The people bowed down and prayed to the golden idol.

But Shadrach, Meshach, and Abednego did not bow down. They kept on standing. They would not pray to this false god.

Some of the king's men saw them. They told the king, "Shadrach, Meshach, and Abednego did not obey your orders. They did not pray to your god."

This made the king angry. He sent for the three men right away.

He told them, "If you don't pray to my god, you will burn in my hot furnace. Do you think your God can save you from the fire?"

Shadrach, Meshach, and Abednego said, "Our God can save us. But no matter what happens, we won't bow to your idol."

The king's face turned red with anger. He told his men, "Heat the furnace seven times hotter! Tie up Shadrach, Meshach, and Abednego. Throw them into the furnace."

The fire burned hot. It burned very, very hot—so hot that it killed the soldiers who threw the men into the furnace.

A little later the king looked into the furnace.

He shouted, "What happened? Didn't we throw three men into the furnace? Why do I see four? One of them looks like an angel. They are walking in the fire. They aren't tied up. They aren't hurt a bit!"

The king went near the opening of the hot furnace.

He called, "You servants of the most high God, come out." So Shadrach, Meshach, and Abednego came out of the fire.

Not a hair of their heads was burned. Their clothes didn't even smell like smoke.

The king said, "Praise your God. He sent His angel to save you. There is no other god as great as your God."

Daniel 3

Daniel and the Lions

Daniel was a friend of Shadrach, Meshach, and Abednego. Soldiers also took him from his home to live in the land of Babylon.

One day a new king ruled in Babylon. Daniel worked hard for the king. He was the king's highest official. But he never forgot God.

Each morning, noon, and night Daniel knelt and prayed to God.

Some other officials didn't like Daniel. They tried to find something wrong with his work for the king. But they couldn't.

At last they said, "We need a plan. We need to get Daniel in trouble."

They went to the king. They told him, "We think you should make a law. Tell everyone to pray to you for 30 days. No one may pray to any other god or man.

"Don't let anyone break this law. If they do, throw them into a pit filled with hungry lions."

The king liked this idea.

He made the new law.

Daniel's enemies watched him. They knew he would pray to God. As soon as Daniel knelt to pray, his enemies ran to the king.

They said, "Daniel broke your new law. He asked his God to help him. Put him into the pit of lions."

Now the king was sorry. All day he tried to find a way to save Daniel's life. But the law could not be changed.

That night the king's men threw Daniel into the pit of lions. They covered the way into the pit with a large stone. The king placed his seal on it. Now no person could help Daniel.

The king said to Daniel, "May your God save you."

The king went back to the palace. He was worried about Daniel. He couldn't sleep all night.

The next morning the king hurried to the pit. He called out, "Daniel, was your God able to save you from the lions?"

Daniel answered, "God sent His angel to shut the mouths of the lions. I am not hurt at all."

The king felt so happy! He asked his servants to pull Daniel out of the pit.

The king said, "I want my whole kingdom to love Daniel's God. He is the true God. His power will last forever."

Daniel 6

The Birth of John

Long before Jesus was born, God promised, "Someday I will send a messenger. He will get people ready for the Savior."

Now it was time for the messenger to be born.

God picked Zechariah and Elizabeth to be the parents of this baby.

Zechariah and Elizabeth were very old. They did not have any children. Most people who were that old would not ever have a child. But Zechariah and Elizabeth still wanted a child very much.

Zechariah was a priest. One day it was his turn to go into the temple.

Zechariah was alone in the temple. He was praying.

All at once Zechariah saw an angel standing before him. Zechariah felt afraid.

The angel said, "Don't be afraid, Zechariah. God has heard your prayers. Soon your wife, Elizabeth, will have a baby boy. Name the baby John.

"He will be a great man. He will tell people that the Savior is coming."

Zechariah did not believe the angel. He asked, "How do I know this will happen? My wife and I are both very old."

The angel answered, "God sent me to tell you this good news. But you did not believe me. Now you won't be able to talk until the baby is born."

Then the angel left.

Zechariah went outside. People were waiting for him. They wondered why he stayed in the temple so long.

Zechariah tried to talk, but he was not able to say a word.

Some time later, Zechariah and Elizabeth had a baby boy. How happy they were!

When the baby was eight days old, friends came to visit Zechariah and Elizabeth.

They wanted to help give the baby a name.

The friends said, "Name the baby after his father. Call him Zechariah."

But Elizabeth said, "No, his name is John."

The friends were surprised. They said, "No one in your family is named John."

Then they asked Zechariah, "What do you want to name the baby?"

Zechariah still could not talk. So he asked his friends to give him a writing pad.

Then Zechariah wrote, "His name is John."

Just then Zechariah was able to talk again. He began to praise and thank God.

Zechariah said, "Soon God will send the Savior. This child, John, will tell people to get ready for the Savior."

Luke 1:5-25, 57-80

75

Jesus Is Coming

Long ago God had promised a Savior. Many times He had promised to send Someone to save the world.

Now it was time.

Soon—very soon—the Savior would be born.

God picked Mary to be the Savior's mother.

Mary lived in Nazareth. She loved God. She often prayed to Him.

Mary planned to marry Joseph. He lived nearby and worked as a carpenter.

One day the angel Gabriel came to Mary's house.

The angel said, "Hello, Mary. God loves you. He is with you."

Mary was afraid.

But the angel said, "Don't be afraid, Mary. God loves you very much. He has picked you to be the mother of a Son. Name Him Jesus. He will be great! He will be the Savior of His people."

Mary asked the angel, "But how can this happen? I'm not married yet."

The angel answered, "God will give you His Son. God can do anything."

Mary told the angel, "I want to obey God. I want it to happen just as you said."

Then the angel Gabriel left her.

Mary was so happy! She loved God so much! He was giving her the most wonderful blessing she could dream of.

One day Mary sang a special song of joy. She sang,

"My heart praises God.
I am so happy!
I am not important,
But God has picked me.
I will be the mother of the
    Savior.
God is holy.
He is strong and good.
He has kept His promise.
The Savior will soon be born."

One night Joseph also saw an angel. The angel told Joseph, "Take Mary to be your wife. The Lord will give her a Son. You are to name Him Jesus. Jesus is the promised Savior. He will save His people from their sins."

Joseph did what the angel told him to do. He took Mary to his home, and she became his wife.

Luke 1:26-56
Matthew 1:18-25

The First Christmas

A king ruled the land where Joseph and Mary lived. The king wanted to know how many people lived in His land.

So he told everybody, "Go to the town where your family used to live. Then I will count you."

Mary and Joseph had to go to the town of Bethlehem. It was a long, long trip. But at last they came to the town.

The streets were noisy and filled with people. Everyone needed a place to stay.

Mary and Joseph looked for a room, too. They tried to find a room at the inn. (An inn was a place where travelers could stay at night.)

The innkeeper told them, "I'm sorry. The rooms are full."

At last someone told Joseph, "Here is a stable. You may stay here." (A stable was a place where people kept their cows and sheep.)

That night something wonderful happened in this stable. Jesus was born! Mary became the mother of baby Jesus. She wrapped the baby in long soft cloths.

Joseph put some clean hay into the manger where the animals ate. The manger made a soft bed for baby Jesus.

That same night shepherds were watching their sheep in the fields around Bethlehem.

Suddenly a bright light shone all around them. The shepherds saw an angel standing in the light. They were afraid!

But the angel said, "Don't be afraid. I bring good news and great joy for all people.

"Tonight the Savior was born in Bethlehem. Go and see Him! You will find Him lying in a manger."

Then the sky was filled with many, many angels. They praised God and sang, "Glory be to God on high; and on earth peace, good will toward men."

Then the angels went back to heaven. The sky was quiet and dark again.

The shepherds said, "Let's go to Bethlehem. Let's find this baby!"

And so they did. They found the stable. They found baby Jesus wrapped in cloths and lying in the manger. They found everything just as the angel said.

On the way back to the fields the shepherds saw many people. They told the people, "Listen! We have good news! Jesus the Savior was born tonight!"

Luke 2:1-20

A Star Leads the Way

Some wise men lived in a land far away from Bethlehem.

One night they saw a bright, new star in the sky.

The Wise Men said, "Look at that star! The new King of the Jews has been born. Let's go see Him!"

The trip took many, many days. But at last the Wise Men came to the city of Jerusalem.

The Wise Men asked, "Where is the baby who will be the new King? We saw His star in the East. We want to pray to Him."

King Herod heard this.

He said to himself, "I am king. I will not let anyone take my place. I will kill this baby."

Then Herod asked some teachers, "Where will the Savior be born?"

They said, "In Bethlehem. That's what the Bible says."

So Herod told the Wise Men, "The baby King is in Bethlehem. Go and find Him. Then come back and tell me where He lives. I want to pray to Him too."

(Herod told a lie. He really wanted to kill Jesus.)

The Wise Men went on to Bethlehem. They saw the star again. It led them to the house where Jesus lived.

The Wise Men felt so happy when they saw Jesus! They prayed to Him. They gave Him gold and other rich gifts.

That night God told them, "Do not go back to Herod."

So they went back to their own country another way.

Then God sent an angel to Joseph.

The angel told Joseph, "Herod wants to kill Jesus. Take the child and His mother to Egypt. Stay there until I tell you to come home."

Joseph obeyed God right away. He woke up Mary. He helped her put warm blankets around the baby Jesus. Then they hurried away to the land of Egypt.

King Herod waited and waited for the Wise Men to come back. But they did not come.

This made Herod very angry. He told his soldiers, "Go to Bethlehem. Kill all the baby boys."

The soldiers did what Herod said. They went to Bethlehem. They killed the baby boys. How the mothers cried!

But the soldiers did not kill Jesus. When the soldiers got to Bethlehem, Jesus was safe.

He was far away in Egypt.

Later, Joseph had another dream. This time the angel said, "You may go home now. It is safe. King Herod is dead."

So Joseph took Jesus and Mary back to Nazareth.

Matthew 2

Jesus in
the Temple

Jesus grew up in Nazareth. He grew stronger and wiser.

God loved His Son Jesus—and people did, too.

Jesus lived with Mary and Joseph. Every year Mary and Joseph went to Jerusalem for the Feast of the Passover.

Jesus did not go with them. He was still too small. So He stayed behind in Nazareth.

At the Passover feast the people went to the temple. There they prayed to God and ate special food.

One day Jesus became old enough to go to the Passover feast. He was 12 years old.

How happy Jesus must have been when He saw Jerusalem for the first time!

The feast lasted seven days. Then everyone started back home.

Many people walked along the road. Mary and Joseph walked along with other parents.

Many of the children did not walk with their parents. They walked with other children.

Mary and Joseph did not see Jesus all day, but they did not worry. They thought He was walking with His friends.

But that night Mary and Joseph began to look for Jesus. They asked their friends, "Have you seen Jesus?"

No one had seen Jesus all day. Now Mary and Joseph were worried. They went all the way back to Jerusalem, looking for Him.

For three days Mary and Joseph looked and looked for Jesus.

They looked along the road. They looked in the streets. They looked everywhere.

At last Mary and Joseph looked for Jesus in the temple.

There He was! Jesus was sitting with the teachers in the temple. He was listening to them. He was asking them questions.

The teachers were surprised at the good answers Jesus gave to their questions.

Mary asked Jesus, "Son, why did You stay here? Your father and I have looked all over Jerusalem for You.

"We were so worried."

Jesus answered, "Why did you look for Me? Didn't you know where I would be? Didn't you know that I would be in My Father's house?"

Then Jesus went back home with Mary and Joseph. He obeyed them all the time. And He kept growing taller and stronger and wiser.

Luke 2:41-52

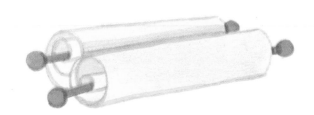

The Baptism of Jesus

John was the son God gave to Elizabeth and Zechariah.

When John grew up, he began his special work. He began to tell people to get ready for the Savior.

John went into the desert to preach to the people. John wore clothes made of camel's hair. He wore a leather belt around his waist. He ate grasshoppers and wild honey.

Many people came to hear John preach.

John told them, "You are all sinners—every one of you. Turn away from your sins. Turn to God. Ask God to forgive your sins. Be baptized and receive God's forgiveness."

People walked up hills and down valleys to hear John.

Many believed John's message from God. These people wanted to be baptized. They wanted God to forgive their sins.

So John baptized them. He baptized them in the Jordan River. John baptized so many people that they called him *John the Baptizer.*

Some people thought John was the Christ—the Savior God had promised long ago.

But John told them, "I am not the Christ. He is much greater than I. I am not good enough to even carry His sandals. I baptize with water. But He will baptize you with the Holy Spirit."

A little later Jesus came to John.

Jesus was about 30 years old. It was time for Him to begin His work as the Savior.

Jesus found John at the Jordan River. Jesus asked John to baptize Him.

But John said, "I need to be baptized by You. But You want me to baptize You?"

Jesus said, "God wants it this way."

So John baptized Jesus.

After Jesus was baptized, He came out of the water. Then the sky above Him opened up.

The Holy Spirit came down in the form of a dove and rested on Jesus. Then a voice came from heaven.

The voice said, "You are My own dear Son. I am pleased with You."

Now John was sure that Jesus was the promised Savior.

Matthew 3
Mark 1
Luke 3
John 1

Jesus Calls the Disciples

The next day John the Baptizer was talking with two of his friends.

They saw Jesus walk by.

John looked at Jesus.

Then he told his friends, "There is the Lamb of God."

Then John's friends followed Jesus. They wanted to learn more about Him.

Jesus saw them and asked, "What are you looking for?"

They answered, "Teacher, where do You live?"

Jesus said, "Come and see."

So they went with Jesus.

They talked with Him for a long time.

One of these men was Andrew. As soon as he left Jesus, he went to find his brother.

He said, "Simon! I have found the Savior!"

Andrew took Simon to see Jesus. They talked, and Simon believed what Jesus told him.

Jesus even gave Simon a new name. He called him Peter.

The next day Jesus met Philip. Jesus said to him, "Follow Me."

Philip was glad to follow Jesus. He wanted his friend Nathanael to know about Jesus too.

So Philip told Nathanael, "God's promise in the Bible has come true! I have found the Savior. His name is Jesus of Nazareth."

Nathanael did not know if he could believe Philip. He asked, "Can anything good come out of Nazareth?"

Philip said, "Come and see." Then Philip brought Nathanael to Jesus.

Jesus told Nathanael, "Before Philip called you, I saw you under the fig tree."

Nathanael answered, "Now I believe. Now I know that You are the Son of God!"

Later on Jesus went by a big lake. There He saw Peter and Andrew again. He saw them throw a net into the water. They were trying to catch some fish.

Jesus called, "Follow Me. I will make you fishers of men."

Right away they got out of their boat and went with Jesus. They learned how to help Him with His work.

Jesus also called other men to be His disciples.

Soon Jesus had 12 disciples. These men went all over the land with Jesus.

They listened and helped as He taught the people. They were His special friends.

John 1:35-51
Matthew 4:18-22

The Wedding at Cana

One day there was a wedding in Cana. Mary, the mother of Jesus, went to the wedding. So did Jesus and some of His disciples.

After the wedding there was a wedding feast. In those days a wedding feast lasted many days.

Many friends of the bride and groom came to the wedding feast. They ate good food. They drank good wine. They talked with each other. The people were happy.

After a while Mary saw that the wine was gone. She knew this would make her friends unhappy. So Mary went to Jesus for help.

Mary told Jesus, "Our friends are out of wine."

Jesus answered, "I know, Mother. Leave everything to Me. But wait until the right time comes."

Mary felt sure Jesus would help the bride and groom.

So she told the servants, "Do whatever Jesus tells you to do."

Six large stone jars stood nearby. They were water jars. Servants poured water out of these jars so that people could wash their hands and feet.

Jesus told the servants, "Fill the jars with water."

So the servants filled all six jars to the very top.

Then Jesus told them, "Pour some water out of one of the jars. Take it to the man in charge of the feast."

The servants took the water to the man in charge. He tasted it.

But it wasn't water any more. It was the best wine he had ever tasted.

The man in charge told the bride and groom, "Other people serve their best wine first. Then they serve the poor wine. But you have saved the best wine of all until now."

The bride and groom did not know what had happened. They had not saved any wine at all.

But the servants knew. They had put water into the jars. And they had poured out wine.

They knew Jesus had changed the water into wine.

This was the first time Jesus showed His glory to people.

It was His first miracle.

His disciples saw what He did. They believed in Him.

They believed that Jesus was the Son of God.

John 2:1-12

Jesus Heals a Paralyzed Man

Four men carried another man down the street on a small bed. He was their friend. They were taking their friend to see Jesus.

The friend could not walk. Someone had to feed and dress him. All day long he had to lie on the small bed. He was very sick, and no doctor could heal him.

The four friends heard that Jesus was in their town.

They knew Jesus had power to heal sick people. So they wanted to ask Jesus to heal their friend.

The men took their friend to the house where Jesus was preaching. At last they got close to the house. They could hear Jesus talking, but they could not see Him.

The men tried to go into the house. But they could not get in. Every room of the house was full. A big crowd stood by the door.

Even the street was crowded. Everyone wanted to see Jesus.

Then the four men saw a stairway on the side of the house. They thought, "The roof is flat. Maybe we can get in that way!" So up they went to the roof.

They made a hole in the roof, right above where Jesus stood. Then they tied a rope to each corner of their friend's bed.

Slowly, slowly, slowly, they let the bed down through the hole. Soon the sick man lay right in front of Jesus.

Jesus saw that the man was sick. He also saw the faith in his heart. Jesus was happy to see how much the man believed in Him.

So Jesus told the man, "My friend, I forgive your sins."

Some people nearby heard Jesus.

They thought, "Who does Jesus think He is? Only God can forgive sins."

They did not believe that Jesus was God's Son.

Jesus knew their thoughts.

He said, "I will show you that I can forgive sins. I will make this sick man well. I have God's power to forgive. I have God's power to heal."

Jesus turned to the sick man and said, "Get up, pick up your bed, and go home."

At once the man stood up. He could walk and jump and bend. He could turn and hop and stretch.

He picked up his small bed and went home. The man was very happy, and he praised God.

Many people saw this miracle. They saw Jesus make the man well.

They were surprised and said, "Praise God! Praise Him always! This is the most wonderful thing we have ever seen!"

Mark 2:1-12
Luke 5:17-26

Jesus Heals a Centurion's Servant

Jesus went all over Galilee. He preached God's Good News to people everywhere.

Sometimes He taught in churches and sometimes on hilltops.

Jesus also healed many people. He took away their sickness and pain.

News about Jesus spread far and wide. Soon people all over the land knew about Him.

Many sick people came to Jesus to be healed. Large crowds followed Jesus everywhere.

One day Jesus came to a town near the Sea of Galilee.

An army officer in the town was very sad. His servant—a very special servant—was sick. The captain was afraid his servant would die.

The captain heard that Jesus was coming. So the captain sent some church leaders to see Him.

They hurried off.

Soon the church leaders found Jesus.

They begged, "Please come and heal the captain's servant. He is very sick. We love the captain very much. He has done many good things for us. He even helped build our church. Please come and help."

Quickly, Jesus went with the church leaders. They hurried to the captain's house.

They were almost there when some friends ran out to them.

They said, "The captain sent us to You. He says he is not worthy to see You himself. He says he does not deserve to have You come to his house. He knows You can heal his servant from right here. Just say the words, and his servant will be well."

Jesus was amazed. The captain's faith was very strong!

A crowd was following behind Jesus.

Jesus turned to the people and said, "I have never found anyone in all of Israel with faith this strong."

Then Jesus told the captain's friends, "The captain believed I would heal his servant. Go back home now. The servant is well."

The captain's friends went back to his house. They saw the servant standing up.

He was well again.

He had been healed at the very same time Jesus had said, "The servant is well."

Matthew 8:5-13
Luke 7:1-10

Jesus Stops a Storm

One day a big crowd of people stood by the Sea of Galilee. They listened to Jesus teach.

The crowd grew and grew.

Soon the people in the back could not see Jesus. And they could not hear Him.

Jesus saw a boat floating in the water. He got into the boat. Now the people could all see His face. Everyone could hear His voice.

Jesus told the people about the kingdom of God. The people listened to all of His words.

They stayed and listened to Jesus all day.

At the end of the day Jesus told His disciples, "Let's row to the other side of the lake."

The disciples stepped into the boat with Jesus.

They began to row.

Jesus went to the back of the boat. He lay down to rest.

The lake was quiet and calm. The boat rocked gently. Jesus soon fell asleep.

Suddenly a bad storm blew across the lake. Strong winds howled. The sky turned black. Dark clouds covered the stars.

The waves got bigger and bigger. Lots of water splashed into the boat.

The disciples tried to row. But the wild waves tossed the little boat up and down.

More water rushed in. Soon the bottom of the boat was filled with water.

The disciples thought, "We're sinking. We will all drown!"

So they went to the back of the boat to wake Jesus. They shouted, "Save us, Lord! Save us before we all drown!"

Jesus stood up. He spoke to the wind and the waves. He said to them, "Peace! Be still!"

The waves stopped tossing. The wind stopped blowing. Stars shone in a clear sky. The lake was calm again. It was perfectly quiet.

Jesus turned to His disciples.

He looked at them and said, "Why are you so afraid? Don't you believe in Me? Don't you know that I can always help you?"

The disciples looked at each other. They were amazed.

They said, "How does Jesus have such power? Even the winds and waves obey Him."

Matthew 8:23-27
Mark 4:35-41
Luke 8:22-25

Jesus Feeds 5,000 People

Many people came to Jesus. They listened to Him preach. They asked Him questions. Sick people came to be healed.

Jesus and His disciples were very busy.

Jesus told His disciples, "Let's go some place where we can be alone and rest awhile."

So they got into a boat and crossed the lake.

But some of the people saw them leave. So they began to walk all the way around the lake to wait for Jesus.

When Jesus got to that side of the lake, He saw the crowd of people.

Jesus spoke to the crowd. He healed many sick people.

All day Jesus helped the people. At last it grew late. Everyone was hungry.

The disciples came up to Jesus. They told Him, "It is getting late. This is a lonely place. There is no food here. Send the people away. Let them go to nearby farms and towns to buy food."

But Jesus said, "They don't have to leave. You give them something to eat."

The disciples answered, "How can we? Look at all the people. We would need lots of food. We don't have enough money to buy that much food."

Jesus said, "Go see how much food is here."

The disciples answered, "One boy here has five loaves of bread and two small fish. But that won't feed all these people!"

Jesus said, "Tell the people to sit down."

Everyone sat down on the green grass. About 5,000 men were there. They waited to see what Jesus was going to do.

Jesus took the bread and fish. He looked up to heaven and thanked God for the food.

Then He broke the five loaves of bread and the two fish into pieces. He gave the food to the disciples, and they gave it to the people.

There was plenty of food. Jesus made it enough for all those many, many people. Everyone ate all they wanted.

Then Jesus told His disciples, "Pick up all the food that is left. We don't want to waste any."

So the disciples picked up all the food that was left over. They filled 12 baskets with the fish and bread that was left.

The people were amazed. They said, "Jesus surely is the Savior whom God promised to send."

Matthew 14:13-21
Mark 6:33-44
Luke 9:11-17
John 6:1-13

Jesus Teaches the Disciples to Pray

One day Jesus was praying to His Father in heaven.

When Jesus stopped praying, the disciples came to Him.

They said, "Lord, please teach us to pray."

Jesus answered, "When you pray, say this:

Our Father who art in
   heaven.
Hallowed be Thy name.
Thy kingdom come.
Thy will be done on earth
   as it is in heaven.
Give us this day
   our daily bread.
And forgive us our trespasses,
   as we forgive those
   who trespass against us.
And lead us not into
   temptation,
But deliver us from evil.
For Thine is the kingdom
   and the power
   and the glory
   forever and ever.
   Amen."

Then Jesus told His disciples a story. He wanted them to be sure that God would hear their prayers. He wanted them to trust God to answer their prayers.

Jesus said, "A man went to his friend's house. It was very late at night.

"The man knocked on the door of his friend's house. He asked, 'Friend, could I have some bread? A visitor has come to see me. And I don't have food for him.'

"The friend answered, 'Don't bother me. The door is locked. My children and I are in bed. I can't get up and give you anything.'

"But the man kept asking. Again and again he knocked on the door of his friend's house. Again and again he asked his friend for some bread. At last the friend got up and gave him the bread."

Jesus told His disciples what the story meant.

Jesus said, "You are like that man. God is your friend. You can pray to Him any time. He will always answer.

"Ask, and it will be given to you. Seek, and you will find. Knock, and the door will be opened for you.

"Would a father give his son a snake when he asks for a fish? Would he give him a scorpion when he asks for an egg?

"Even sinful fathers give good things to their children. You can be sure, then, that your Father in heaven will give good things to you.

"Your Father in heaven will also give you the best gift of all. He will give the Holy Spirit to anyone who asks Him."

Matthew 6:9-15
Luke 11:1-13

Jesus Raises a Little Girl from the Dead

A man named Jairus lived by the Sea of Galilee. He and his wife had a daughter who was 12 years old.

One day their daughter got sick. Jairus and his wife could not help her. The doctors could not help her.

The girl just lay on her bed. Each day she grew weaker and weaker. Jairus was afraid she would die.

One day Jesus came close to the home of Jairus.

Jairus believed Jesus could heal his daughter.

So he rushed out to meet Jesus. He kneeled down in front of Jesus. He begged Jesus to help him.

Jairus cried, "Please come with me. My daughter is dying. I know You can make her well."

Jesus started walking home with Jairus. While they were on the way, some friends came to Jairus.

They told him, "Don't bother Jesus any more. Your little daughter has died."

Jairus felt so sad. It was too late! He had gone to Jesus too late!

Then Jesus said, "Don't be afraid, Jairus. Just believe. I can still help you."

They went on to Jairus' house. Many people filled the house. They all were crying because the girl had died.

Jesus asked, "Why are you crying? The girl is not dead. She's only sleeping."

The people laughed at Jesus and made fun of Him. They knew the girl was dead.

Jesus told all the people to leave the house. Then He went into the girl's room. He took Jairus, his wife, and three disciples with Him.

Jesus took the girl's hand.

He said, "Get up, little girl!"

At once the girl opened her eyes. She stood up and walked around the room.

Jesus said, "Give her something to eat."

Jairus and his wife were so happy and so surprised! Jesus had brought their little girl back to life!

Matthew 9:18-26
Mark 5:21-43
Luke 8:40-56

The Forgiving Father

God our Father loves us very much. He sent Jesus, His only Son, into the world. Jesus came to take away our sins.

One day Jesus told this story. The story shows how much God loves us.

This is the story Jesus told:

Once there was a man who had two sons.

The younger son said, "Father, give me my share of your money. I don't want to wait until you die. I want my money now."

The father was sad. But he gave the money to his son.

Then the son left. He went far away. There he wasted his money on sinful things.

At last his money was gone. He could not even buy food.

Then he found a job. He took care of the pigs on a farm. The son felt so hungry! He wanted to eat the food the pigs ate!

Now he began to think about his kind and good father.

He said to himself, "My father's servants have more food than they can eat. And here I am starving. I will go back to my father. I will tell him, 'Father, I have sinned. I don't deserve to be called your son. Make me one of your servants.'"

So the young man started for home.

When he was still far away from the house, his father saw him. He ran to his son and threw his arms around him.

The son said, "Father, I have sinned against God and against you. I don't deserve to be called your son."

But the father called his servants. He said, "Hurry! Bring the best coat and put it on him. Put a ring on his finger and shoes on his feet. Get a feast ready! My lost son has been found!"

Later the older son came home from the fields. He heard music.

He asked a servant, "What's going on?"

The servant said, "Your brother has come home. Your father is giving a feast."

The older brother was angry. He would not go into the house. His father came out and begged him to join the party.

But the older son said, "I have worked for you all these years. I always did what you said. But you never gave me a party like this. Now my sinful brother comes back, and you give him a big feast."

His father answered, "Son, you have always been with me. All I have is yours. You know that. But today we must be happy. Your brother was dead, but now he is alive. He was lost, but now he has been found."

Luke 15:11-32

How Two Men Prayed

In Jesus' day the Pharisees thought they were better than other people. They kept the rules God gave to Moses.

They also kept many other rules. But these were not God's rules. These were rules the Pharisees made up.

The Pharisees had rules for washing hands. They had rules to tell how far they could walk on the Sabbath Day. They had rules against talking to "bad" people. The Pharisees had lots and lots of rules.

But the Pharisees forgot one important rule. They forgot God's rule of love.

The Pharisees looked fine on the outside, but their hearts were far from God. The Pharisees obeyed their own rules, but they did not have joy and faith and love in their hearts.

One day Jesus told a story to show the Pharisees that they were wrong.

Jesus said:

One day two men went to the temple to pray. One was a Pharisee. The other was a tax collector.

The Pharisee stood alone in the middle of the temple. He wanted everyone to see him.

The Pharisee prayed, "Thank You, God, for making me so good. I am not as sinful as other people. I don't steal. I don't cheat.

"I'm so glad I am not a sinner like that tax collector over there. I keep all the rules. I also give a lot of money to poor people."

The tax collector stood far away by himself. He hung his head because he was ashamed. He hit his chest with his hand to show that he was sorry for his sins.

The tax collector said, "God, forgive me. I am a sinner."

Now Jesus had finished His story.

Then Jesus told the people, "The tax collector went home forgiven. The Pharisee was not forgiven.

"People who brag and think they are good do NOT get God's love and forgiveness. Those who are sorry for their sins and ask God to forgive them DO get His forgiveness.

"I tell you, trust and believe in God. Believe that He will forgive all your sins."

Luke 18:9-14

Jesus Heals a Blind Man

Jesus and His disciples were going to Jerusalem. They wanted to be in Jerusalem for the Passover feast.

Jesus knew that this would be a special Passover feast. It would be His last Passover. His time on earth was almost over.

Jesus wanted His disciples to know what was going to happen.

So Jesus stopped and said, "Long ago God's prophets told about Me. They told how I would save the world.

"Soon those things will happen. Those things will happen in Jerusalem. People will make fun of me. They will beat me and kill me. But three days later I will rise to life again."

The disciples listened to Jesus' words. But they did not understand them. Still they went along with Jesus to Jerusalem.

Jesus and His disciples walked on down the road. They came to the city of Jericho. A blind man sat by the side of the road. He begged for money.

The blind man heard many voices. A large crowd was walking by.

The blind man asked, "What's going on?"

Some people told him, "Jesus is walking by."

The blind man knew about Jesus. He knew Jesus could make him see.

The blind man shouted, "Jesus! Have mercy on me!"

Some people did not want a poor blind man to bother Jesus. So they told him, "Be quiet!"

But he shouted even louder, "Jesus! Have mercy on me!"

Jesus heard the blind man call. He stopped and said, "Bring the man to Me."

People told the blind man, "Stand up! We have good news! Jesus is calling for you."

The blind man jumped to his feet. The people led him to Jesus.

Jesus asked, "What do you want Me to do?"

The blind man answered, "Sir, I want to see again."

Jesus said, "Then you will see. Your faith has made you well."

At once the man could see again. He could see blue sky and green grass. He could see the face of Jesus smiling at him.

The man felt so happy! He thanked Jesus and followed Him down the road.

Mark 10:46-52
Luke 18:35-43

Jesus Rides into Jerusalem

Jesus and His disciples were on their way to Jerusalem.

A large crowd followed them. The people had seen Jesus heal the blind man. Now they hoped Jesus would be their new king.

At last Jesus got close to Jerusalem. Then He stopped.

Jesus told two of His disciples, "Go into town. There you will find a donkey. Untie it and bring it to me.

"A man might ask you, 'Why are you taking the donkey?'

"Tell him, 'The Lord needs it.' Then the man will let you have the donkey."

The disciples went into town. They found the donkey just as Jesus had told them.

The disciples untied it.

The owner came out and asked, "Why are you untying my donkey?"

The disciples answered, "The Lord needs it."

Then the owner said, "Go ahead and take it."

The disciples led the donkey back to Jesus. They put their coats on its back.

Then Jesus climbed on.

He rode the little donkey into Jerusalem.

Jerusalem was full of people. Many of them had come for the Passover. The people heard that Jesus was coming, so they ran to meet Him.

Many, many people went to meet Jesus. Some of them put their coats on the road. Others cut palm branches and laid them on the road.

The people wanted Jesus to be their King. They made a carpet for their King to ride on. They made a carpet of coats and palm branches for Jesus.

Some people ran in front of Jesus. Some walked behind Him. They all shouted, "Praise God. Hosanna! Hosanna to the Son of David! God bless the One who is coming in the name of the Lord! Hosanna in the highest!"

The people went into Jerusalem with Jesus. They waved their palm branches. And they shouted praises to Jesus.

Other people heard the praises. They heard the shouting.

They asked, "Who is this Man?"

The crowds shouted back, "This is Jesus of Nazareth!"

Some Pharisees watched the happy crowd. They heard the shouting, too.

The Pharisees had become enemies of Jesus. They did not like the things they saw and heard.

The Pharisees asked, "How can we stop Jesus? The whole world is following Him. We must get rid of Him."

Matthew 21:1-11
Mark 11:1-11
Luke 19:29-44
John 12:12-19

The Second Coming of Jesus

One day Jesus sat on a hill near Jerusalem. His disciples asked Him about the end of the world, the time when Jesus will come again.

They asked, "When will You come back? What will happen then?"

Then Jesus told them about His second coming.

Jesus' second coming will not be like the first coming.

At the first coming Jesus was born in a stable. He came as a poor little baby.

But when He comes again, Jesus will come in all His glory. He will take those who believe in Him home with Him to heaven.

Jesus said, "You will hear loud trumpets. You will see My angels. You will see My power and glory.

"No one knows when I will come. So watch and be ready."

(Do you know how to be ready when Jesus comes? Ask Jesus every day to forgive your sins. Believe that He loves you and died for you. Then you will also come to love Him more and more. Then you will be ready for His second coming.)

Then Jesus told His disciples about the Last Day.

Jesus said:

I will sit as King on a throne. All the people in the world will stand before Me. All those who believe in Me will stand on My right side. All the others will stand on My left side.

I will tell those on My right, "Come to heaven with Me. I was hungry, and you fed Me. I was thirsty, and you gave Me a drink. I was all alone, and you took Me into your homes. I was naked, and you gave Me clothes. I was sick, and you took care of Me. I was in prison, and you visited Me."

And they will answer, "Lord, when did we do that?"

I will say to them, "Every time you were kind to one of My brothers or sisters, you were kind to Me."

(The brothers and sisters of Jesus are all those who believe in Him.)

Then I will tell those on My left, "Go away from Me! I was hungry and thirsty. I was all alone. I was naked. I was sick and in prison. But you never helped Me."

They will answer, "But, Lord, we never saw You."

Then I will say to them, "Every time you did not help one of My brothers or sisters, you did not help Me."

Then these people will be punished forever.

But the people who believe in Me will live in joy forever.

Matthew 24—25

The Last Supper

Jesus wanted to eat His last Passover meal with His disciples.

So along a dusty street He walked with them. They went to a large upstairs room. But before they went in, they took off their sandals. That's what people did in those days. Then a servant would wash their dirty feet.

But there was no servant at this place. And not one of the disciples said, "Let ME be the servant."

So all the disciples sat down at the table with dirty feet.

Then Jesus started to wash the disciples' feet. How surprised the disciples were!

Peter told Jesus, "Don't wash my feet. This isn't a job for You, Lord."

Jesus said, "If you don't let Me wash you, you can't be My disciple."

Jesus washed the feet of all the disciples. Then He went back to the table and sat down.

Jesus said, "Do you know why I did that? I wanted to teach you how to live. I am your Lord, but I served each of you. Now you must serve one another."

Then Jesus and His disciples started to eat the Passover meal.

Jesus told them, "Tonight one of you will tell My enemies where to find Me. They will arrest Me."

The disciples were surprised and afraid when Jesus said that.

They did not know what Judas had done. Judas was a disciple of Jesus. But he loved money too much. Jesus' enemies had paid Judas 30 pieces of silver. Judas had promised to help them catch Jesus.

Jesus knew what Judas planned. But the other disciples didn't.

Soon Judas got up. He went to help Jesus' enemies.

During the meal Jesus did a special thing. He broke some bread and gave it to the disciples. He said, "Take, eat. This is My body, which is given for you."

Then He passed a cup of wine. He said, "Drink it, all of you. This is My blood, which I shed to take away your sins."

Jesus told His disciples to eat bread and drink wine in this special way often. He said, "Do this to remember Me."

This special meal is the Lord's Supper.

Today, too, Jesus gives His disciples His body and His blood in this supper. And He reminds us of His suffering and death for all our sins.

Matthew 26:17-29
Mark 14:12-25
Luke 22:7-30
John 13:1-32

Jesus in Gethsemane

After supper Jesus took His disciples to the Garden of Gethsemane.

On the way He told them, "All of you will run away when My enemies come."

Peter was surprised. He said, "I will never leave You!"

Jesus told him, "Three times tonight you will say that you don't know Me. Then the rooster will crow."

Peter answered, "I will die with You before I do that."

They got to the garden.

Jesus told His disciples, "Stay here while I pray."

Then Jesus took Peter, James, and John with Him into the garden.

Jesus told them, "I feel so sad. I could almost die from sadness. Stay here and watch with Me."

Jesus walked on alone. He fell to the ground and prayed, "O My Father, please save Me. Is there another way to save people from their sin? Then keep Me from having to suffer and die for the sins of the whole world. But do what You want, not what I want."

Jesus came back to the three disciples. They were sleeping.

Jesus woke them and asked, "Can't you watch with Me for even one hour? Please stay awake and pray, so you won't fall into sin."

Jesus walked away again.

He prayed, "Father, I will do anything You want Me to do."

Jesus came back to Peter, James, and John. They were asleep again.

Jesus went to pray for a third time. God sent an angel to help Jesus feel strong.

Then Jesus went back to His disciples.

He told them, "Get up. It is time for My enemies to take Me away. Look, here they come now."

The disciples woke up. They saw Judas walking toward them.

A crowd of men followed behind. They carried bright lights and clubs and swords.

Judas stepped up to Jesus and kissed Him. Now the enemies knew which person was Jesus.

Jesus looked at Judas sadly. He asked, "Judas, are you helping My enemies by giving Me a kiss?"

Then the enemies came up to Jesus and arrested Him.

The enemies led Jesus out of the garden. The disciples thought the enemies might take them, too. So they all ran away.

Matthew 26:30-56
Mark 14:26-52
Luke 22:31-53
John 18:1-11

Peter Denies Jesus

The enemies of Jesus took Him to the high priest's house. Many church leaders came there for a meeting.

The high priest wanted Jesus to be killed. But first he needed a reason to kill Jesus.

Peter followed far behind. He wanted to see where they took Jesus. He wanted to know what they would do with Him.

Peter walked into the yard to watch and listen.

Inside the house, people told the high priest bad things about Jesus. But all these things were lies. The high priest still could not find a reason to kill Jesus.

At last the high priest asked Jesus, "What do You say for Yourself?"

Jesus didn't say a word.

Then the high priest asked, "Are You the Son of God?"

Jesus answered, "I am."

Now the high priest got angry. He tore his clothes and said, "What a terrible thing to say! Jesus is lying about God. What do you think we should do with Jesus?"

The church leaders shouted, "He should be killed!"

Then the guards hit Jesus, spit on Him, and made fun of Him.

Peter was still waiting in the yard. He sat by the warm fire with servants and guards.

A servant girl looked right at Peter. She asked, "Weren't you with Jesus?"

Peter was afraid. They might want to kill him, too. So he answered, "No, I wasn't there."

Peter moved away from the fire. But another servant girl asked, "Aren't you one of Jesus' disciples?"

Peter lied, "No, I am not! I don't know what you're talking about."

Later someone else said, "I saw you with Jesus in the garden. I can tell that you are His disciple. You talk like the people from Galilee."

Now Peter felt very scared. He shouted, "I don't even know that Man!"

Just then the rooster crowed.

Then Peter remembered Jesus' words. Jesus had said, "Peter, tonight you will say that you do not know Me."

Now Peter became very sad. He ran out of the yard. Tears rolled down his face. Peter cried and cried.

He was so sorry. Three times he had told people that he did not know Jesus!

Matthew 26:57-75
Mark 14:53-72
Luke 22:54-71
John 18:12-27

Jesus Before Pilate

Early the next morning the high priest and church leaders took Jesus to Pontius Pilate. He was the only ruler who could order people to be put to death.

Pilate asked, "What wrong did this Man do?"

They said, "He has caused all kinds of trouble. He has told people not to pay taxes to your king. He even says that He is the King."

Jesus didn't say a word. He stood calm and quiet.

Pilate went into his palace. He called Jesus and asked Him, "Are You the King of the Jews?"

Jesus answered, "My kingdom is not of this world."

Pilate asked again, "Are You a king then?"

Jesus said, "Yes, I am a king. But I am not like the kings in this world. I came into the world to tell people the truth. Everyone who believes the truth is in My kingdom."

Pilate answered, "What is truth?"

Then Pilate went out to the people again. By now a big crowd stood outside the palace.

Pilate wanted to let Jesus go, so he told them, "Each Passover I set free any prisoner you choose. Do you want Jesus or Barabbas?"

Barabbas was a robber. Pilate felt sure the people would pick Jesus.

But the priests and church leaders had told the crowd to pick Barabbas. So the people shouted, "Barabbas! We want Barabbas to go free!"

Pilate asked, "What shall I do with Jesus?"

"Crucify Him!" the crowd shouted.

Pilate went back inside. He told his soldiers to beat Jesus.

The soldiers hit Jesus until He was bloody. They put a crown of thorns on His head. They put a purple robe on Him. Then they spit on Him and laughed at Him.

Pilate took Jesus back to the shouting crowd. He was sure they would feel sorry for Him now. Now they would want to let Him go.

But the crowd still shouted, "Crucify Him! Crucify Him!"

At last Pilate gave in to the crowd. He told his soldiers take Jesus and crucify Him.

Matthew 27:1-26
Mark 15:1-15
Luke 23:1-25
John 18:28—19:16

Jesus Is Crucified

The soldiers took Jesus to a hill outside Jerusalem called Calvary.

When they got to the hill, the soldiers put Jesus on the cross. They nailed His hands and feet to the cross.

Many people walked by and made fun of Jesus.

Jesus hurt so much! But He was not angry with the people who nailed Him to the cross.

Jesus prayed for them. He prayed, "Father, forgive them. They don't know what they are doing."

Two robbers hung on crosses next to Jesus. One of them believed in Jesus. This robber was sorry for his sins.

Jesus told him, "Today you will be with Me in heaven."

Then Jesus looked down below Him. He saw His mother standing with John, one of His disciples. Jesus wanted John to take care of His mother.

So Jesus told His mother, "This is your son."

And He told John, "This is your mother."

When Jesus had been on the cross for three hours, it was noon. The sun shone high in the sky.

Suddenly the whole land got as dark as night. It stayed dark for three hours.

All this time Jesus was suffering to pay for the sins of the world. Because of these sins, God let Jesus suffer all alone. This hurt Jesus most of all.

At last Jesus cried, "My God, why have You left Me?"

After that Jesus said, "I am thirsty."

Someone dipped a sponge into sour wine and gave it to Him.

A little later Jesus cried with a loud voice, "It is finished."

Then He said, "Father, into Your hands I give My spirit." And Jesus died.

Then some friends of Jesus took His body from the cross. They wrapped it in cloth and laid it in a grave. They closed the door to the grave with a large stone.

The next morning, Jesus' enemies met with Pilate. They told him, "Jesus said He would rise in three days. Guard His grave. We don't want His disciples to steal His body. They might say He is alive."

So Pilate sent soldiers to guard the grave of Jesus.

Matthew 27:32-66
Mark 15:16-47
Luke 23:33-56
John 19:17-42

The First Easter

It was very early Sunday morning. Soldiers were guarding the grave of Jesus.

All at once the ground shook. A bright shining angel came from heaven. He rolled the stone away from the grave.

The soldiers were very scared. They fell to the ground. Then they ran away.

Some women were walking to the grave that morning. They carried spices to put on Jesus' body.

They asked one another, "Who will roll the big stone away for us?"

But when the women got there, they saw that the stone had been rolled away. And all the soldiers had left.

Mary Magdalene thought someone had taken Jesus. She went to tell Peter and John.

The other women looked into the grave. They saw two angels sitting there.

One angel said, "I know you are looking for Jesus. But He is not here. He has risen just as He said He would. Go and tell His disciples."

At once the women ran to tell the disciples.

Mary Magdalene did not know that Jesus had risen. She told Peter and John that His body was missing.

Peter and John ran to the grave. Mary followed behind.

They saw the cloth Jesus had been wrapped in. It was folded neatly. But they did not see Jesus. And they did not see the angels.

Then Peter and John went home, but Mary stayed by Jesus' grave.

Mary was crying. When she bent over to look inside the grave, she saw two angels.

One of them asked her, "Why are you crying?"

Mary answered, "Jesus is missing. They have taken Him away. I don't know where He is."

Just then Mary turned around. She saw a Man standing behind her. Mary thought He was the gardener.

He asked, "Who are you looking for?"

Mary said, "If you took Jesus away, tell me where you have put Him."

The Man said, "Mary!"

Now Mary knew He was Jesus.

She cried, "Master! My dear Lord!" Now Mary was so happy!

Jesus told her, "Tell My disciples that I am alive."

Matthew 28:1-15
Mark 16:1-13
Luke 24:1-11
John 20:1-18

Jesus Appears to Two Disciples

ater that same Sunday, two men walked toward Emmaus. That town was about seven miles from the city of Jerusalem.

As the men walked down the road, they talked about Jesus. Why did He die? Where was His body? There were so many things they did not know.

Suddenly a Man came up and walked with them. It was Jesus, but they did not know Him.

He asked, "What are you talking about?"

The two men stopped walking. Their faces looked so sad.

One of them asked, "Don't You know what has happened?"

Jesus asked, "What happened?"

They told Him, "Jesus of Nazareth was a wonderful Teacher. He helped many people with His miracles. Everybody loved Him. We hoped He was the Savior.

"But three days ago some of His enemies took Him to Pilate. Then some soldiers nailed Him to a cross, and He died.

"Today, women went to His grave. They could not find His body. They say they saw angels. The angels told them that Jesus is alive.

"Some others also went to His grave, but they did not see Jesus."

Jesus said, "Why don't you believe God's Word? God planned for Jesus to die. That is how He was to save all people from sin.

Now Jesus has risen, and He will go to heaven."

Jesus kept talking with the men. He told them what the Bible says about Jesus.

At last they came to Emmaus. The two men stopped, but Jesus acted as if He would go on.

The men begged Jesus, "Please stay with us. It is very late."

So Jesus went into the house. The men set out food to eat. Jesus picked up the bread and blessed it. He broke it and gave it to them.

Suddenly the two men knew He was Jesus. Just as quickly Jesus went away. They could not see Him anymore.

The men said, "Wasn't it wonderful walking and talking with Him? He made us feel so happy!"

Then the two men got up and hurried all the way back to Jerusalem. They knocked on the door where the disciples were meeting.

The two men said, "Jesus really has risen! We walked with Him. We talked with Him. We even had supper with Him. Jesus is alive!"

Luke 24:13-35

Jesus Appears to Many Disciples

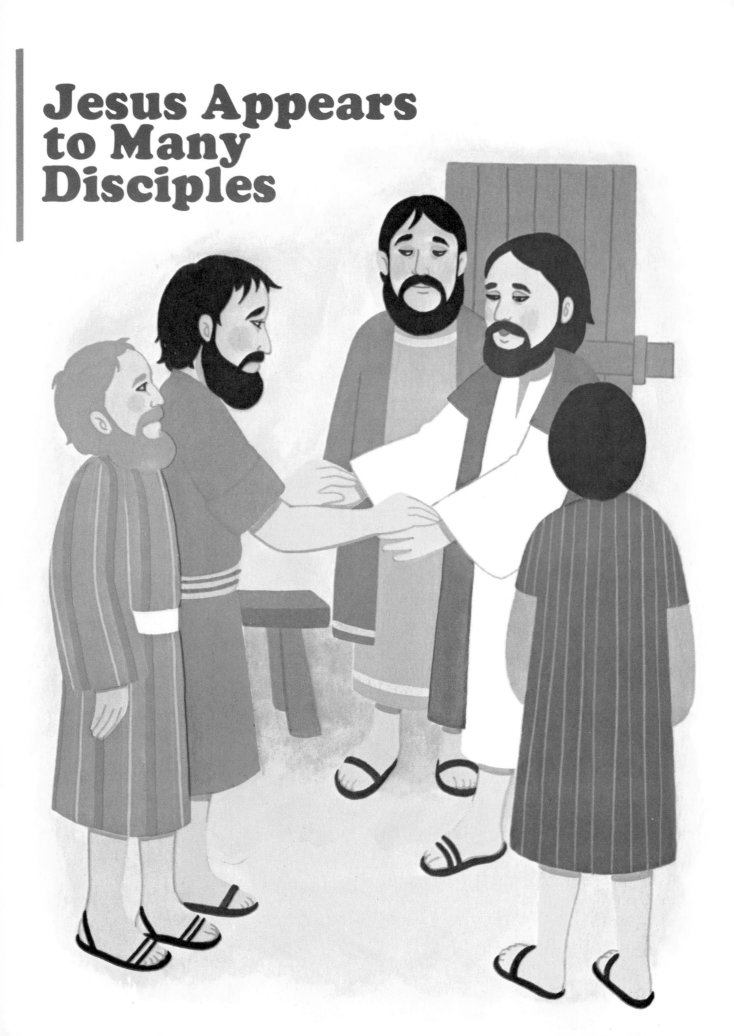

It was very late on Easter Day. The disciples were all meeting together. They locked the door because they were afraid. Maybe the soldiers would kill them, just as they had killed Jesus.

All the disciples except Thomas were together in that room.

Suddenly Jesus Himself stood in the room with them.

He said, "Peace be with you."

The disciples were afraid. They thought He was a ghost.

Jesus asked, "Why are you afraid? I am not a ghost. Ghosts don't have skin and bones. Look at My hands and feet. Feel the places where they nailed Me to the cross."

Then Jesus asked the disciples, "Do you have any thing to eat?"

The disciples gave Him a piece of cooked fish. Jesus ate it.

Then Jesus told them, "My Father sent Me to take away the sins of the world. Now I send you.

"Tell all people what you have seen. I will give you the Holy Spirit. He will help you in your work."

Then Jesus went away.

Now the disciples were sure that Jesus was alive. He had risen from the dead. They couldn't wait to tell Thomas.

Sometime later they saw Thomas. They told him, "We have seen Jesus. He is alive."

But Thomas said, "I don't believe it. I will not believe it until I touch the marks in His hands and on His side."

A week later the disciples were together again. This time Thomas was with them. Again all the doors were locked.

Suddenly Jesus came and stood with them. He said, "Peace be with you."

Jesus looked at Thomas.

Jesus told him, "Put your finger on the marks in My hands. Put your hand in My side. Stop doubting and believe."

Now Thomas was sure Jesus had risen. He said, "My Lord and My God!"

Jesus said, "You believe because you have seen Me. Blessed are those who don't see Me, but still believe in Me."

Luke 24:36-43
John 20:19-29

Jesus Appears at the Sea of Galilee

Seven of Jesus' disciples met by the Sea of Galilee.

Peter said, "I'm going fishing."

The others told him, "We will go with you."

So all seven disciples climbed into a boat. They fished all night. But they did not catch any fish.

At last it was morning. The disciples started back to shore. They saw a Man standing on the beach. It was Jesus. But they could not tell who He was.

Jesus asked them, "Did you catch any fish?"

They answered, "No."

Jesus called, "Throw your net on the other side of the boat. Then you will catch some fish."

The disciples did just what Jesus told them.

Right away they caught lots of fish. Their net was full of fish. It was so full that they could not pull the net back into the boat.

John knew this was a miracle. He said, "That must be Jesus!"

Peter couldn't wait to see Jesus again. He jumped into the water and swam to the shore.

The other disciples followed in the boat.

When they came to the beach, they saw a fire burning. Fish and bread cooked on the fire.

Jesus said, "Bring some of the fish you caught."

Peter pulled the net onto the beach. It was filled with 153 big fish. But still the net was not torn.

Then Jesus said, "Come and eat breakfast."

The seven disciples sat around the fire with Jesus. He gave them bread and fish. The disciples felt so happy to see Him!

Jesus asked Peter, "Peter, do you love Me more than the other disciples do?"

Peter answered, "Yes, Lord. You know that I love You."

Jesus said, "Feed My lambs."

Jesus asked again, "Peter, do you love Me?"

Peter answered, "Yes, Lord. You know that I love You."

Jesus told him, "Take care of My sheep."

Then Jesus asked a third time, "Peter, do you love Me?"

Peter felt sad. Three times Jesus asked him, "Do you love Me?"

Peter said, "Lord, You know everything. You know that I love You."

Jesus said, "Feed My sheep."

John 21:1-17

Jesus Goes Back to Heaven

Jesus stayed on earth 40 days after He rose from the dead. He showed Himself to the disciples many times during these 40 days. Jesus wanted them to be sure that He was really alive.

Jesus told His disciples more about the kingdom of God. The disciples learned why Jesus became a man. They learned why He had to suffer and die and rise again.

Jesus also gave His disciples new work to do.

Jesus told them, "Go to all the people in the whole world. Make them My disciples. Baptize them in the name of the Father, Son, and Holy Spirit. Teach them all about Me. And remember, I will always be with you."

Soon Jesus would go to heaven. The disciples would not see Him anymore. But He would still be near them all the time.

Jesus also promised His disciples a special Gift from heaven. He said, "Stay here in Jerusalem and wait. Wait for My Gift—the Holy Spirit."

Then, one day, Jesus led His disciples out of Jerusalem. They went to a hill near the town of Bethany.

This was a special day. It was time for Jesus to go to heaven. His disciples would not see Him anymore.

Jesus told the disciples, "The Holy Spirit will come to you. You will be filled with God's power. And you will tell people all over the world about Me."

Jesus lifted His hands and blessed the disciples. Then He began to rise from the earth. Higher and higher He went.

The disciples watched Jesus rise in the sky. A cloud floated across the sky. It hid Jesus. Now the disciples could not see Him. But they still looked up at the sky.

Suddenly two angels stood beside the disciples. They were all dressed in white.

The angels said, "Why are you looking up at the sky? Jesus has gone to heaven. But He will come back in the same way you saw Him go."

Then the disciples walked back to Jerusalem. They felt very happy. They knew Jesus was alive. They had watched Him go to heaven. They knew He would come back. And they believed that He would always be with them.

The disciples went to their meeting room. They prayed together. They thanked God for sending His Son.

Matthew 28:16-20
Mark 16:15-20
Luke 24:44-53
Acts 1:1-14

The First Pentecost

The disciples often met in their meeting room in Jerusalem. They prayed there. And they waited for the gift of the Holy Spirit, just like Jesus had told them to.

One day something special happened. All at once the disciples heard a noise.

It sounded like a big windstorm. The noise filled the whole room.

The disciples looked around. They saw flames like fire. The flames sat on the heads of each person in the room.

Then all the disciples were filled with the Holy Spirit. They wanted to tell everyone about Jesus the Savior. They were all able to speak in other languages.

People from all over the world were in Jerusalem at that time. They heard the noise. They came to see what had happened.

The disciples went out and preached to all these people.

When the people heard them, they got excited. They asked, "How do these men know our languages? The disciples are all from Galilee. We are from Asia, Egypt, and Rome. But we can all understand them. What has happened?"

Peter stood before the crowd. He said, "I will tell you what has happened. God has sent us His Holy Spirit.

"Now listen to what God says.

"God sent Jesus to earth. Jesus told about God's love. He helped people with His miracles.

"But you hated Him. You killed Him on a cross.

"Three days later God raised Him to life again. We saw Him with our own eyes. Now He is in heaven with His Father.

"Today He sent His Holy Spirit to us. That is why we can speak in your languages. Now we can tell you about Jesus. Now we can tell you that the One you killed is the Savior sent by God."

The people listened to Peter. They knew they had killed Jesus. Now they felt sorry. So they asked, "What can we do?"

Peter told them, "Be sorry for your sin. Believe in Jesus and be baptized, so your sins may be forgiven. You will also get God's gift—the Holy Spirit."

Many believed Peter's words. About 3,000 people were baptized that very day.

Each day these believers came together to study God's Word.

They shared their food. They helped each other. And they prayed together.

Acts 2

Dorcas Is Raised

Peter told many people in Jerusalem about Jesus.

Then he went to other places. Peter was doing the new work Jesus gave him.

Peter and the disciples were now called *apostles.*

Jesus had chosen the apostles to preach the Good News about Him.

The Holy Spirit always helped Peter.

One time Peter visited some of God's people in Lydda. There he met a man who could not walk. The man had been lying in bed for eight years.

Peter said to him, "Jesus makes you well. Get up from your bed."

At once the man got up. He could walk again.

All the people who lived in the town saw the man.

They knew Jesus had made him well. They began to believe in Jesus.

The city of Joppa was about 10 miles from Lydda. A woman named Dorcas lived there.

Dorcas loved Jesus and believed in Him. Dorcas also loved other people. She made clothes for poor people.
She did many other kind things.

One day Dorcas got sick. Soon she died.

Some friends of Dorcas heard that Peter was nearby.

They sent two men to Peter.

The men said, "Please come quickly and help us."

So Peter left Lydda and went to Joppa. The friends took him to Dorcas' house.

Many people were crying there. They showed Peter the dresses and coats Dorcas had made for them.

Peter asked them all to leave the room. He knelt down and prayed. Then he looked at Dorcas. Peter said, "Get up, Dorcas."

Dorcas opened her eyes. She saw Peter and sat up. Peter took her hand and helped her to stand. He called all her friends. He showed them Dorcas was alive.

People all over Joppa heard what happened. They knew Dorcas had come back to life. And they knew that God gave Peter the power to bring her back to life.

Many people believed in Jesus because of this miracle.

Acts 9:32-43

Peter Is Freed from Prison

King Herod wanted to get rid of the Christians. So one day his soldiers killed James.

Then he put Peter into prison. Herod planned to kill him, too.

Peter's friends did not forget him. They met at Mark's house. Every day they prayed for Peter.

Peter was always chained to two soldiers. Two other soldiers stood outside the door of the prison.

One night Peter was asleep between the two soldiers who were chained to him. He knew Herod planned to kill him the next day.

But Peter was sound asleep.

Suddenly an angel came into the prison. The angel said to Peter, "Get up! Quick!"

Peter woke up. At once his chains fell off. The soldiers did not wake up.

The angel said, "Put on your shoes and coat. Then come with me."

Peter followed the angel. He thought he was dreaming.

They passed the first guards. They passed the second guards. None of them stopped Peter.

At last Peter and the angel came to the iron gate outside the prison. The gate opened all by itself, and they walked out into the street. Then the angel left Peter.

Now Peter knew he wasn't dreaming. He was really free!

Peter hurried to Mark's house.

The door was locked, and Peter's friends were praying inside. Peter knocked on the door.

A servant girl went to the door. Her name was Rhoda.

Peter said, "Please let me in."

Rhoda knew Peter's voice. She became so happy that she forgot to open the door.

Rhoda ran to the others. She told them, "It's Peter! Peter is standing at the door!"

But they would not believe her.

So she said again, "It's Peter! It really is!"

"It can't be," they said. "He is in prison. That must be his angel."

Peter kept knocking.

This time the others went to see. At last they opened the door. Sure enough, it was Peter! They were so excited! Everyone talked at once.

Peter asked them to be quiet. He told them how God had answered their prayers and set him free. He said, "Tell all the other Christians what God has done tonight."

Then Peter left and went to another place.

Acts 12:1-17

Saul Becomes a Christian

Saul followed the rules that the Pharisees made. He hated the Christians. He believed they taught wrong things. Saul wanted to put all Christians into jail.

He said to the high priest, "Let me go to Damascus. I want to look for Christians. I will bring them back to Jerusalem and put them into jail."

So Saul started out for Damascus. He took other men to help him.

They had almost reached the city when a bright light shone from the sky. Saul fell to the ground and covered his eyes.

A voice from heaven called, "Saul, why are you hurting Me?"

Saul asked, "Who are You?"

The voice said, "I am Jesus. Get up and go into the city. You will be told what to do next."

Saul stood up and opened his eyes. But he could not see.

The men with Saul took his hand and led him to Damascus. They took him to a house on Straight Street.

For three days Saul sat alone. He could not see, and he did not eat or drink. But now he did not try to hurt the friends of Jesus. Now he prayed to Jesus.

Ananias was a Christian who lived in Damascus.

One night Jesus told him, "Go to Straight Street. Ask for a man named Saul."

Ananias said, "I have heard about that man. He hates Christians. He wants to put them into prison."

Jesus told him, "I have special work for Saul. I want him to preach about Me. He will suffer great things for Me."

So Ananias went to the house on Straight Street. He placed his hands on Saul. He told him, "Brother Saul, Jesus sent me. He wants you to see again. And He will fill you with the Holy Spirit."

At once Saul could see again.

Then Ananias said, "Jesus chose you for special work. Now He wants to wash away your sins. Stand up and be baptized."

Saul got up and was baptized. He ate some food. He felt strong and ready to work for Jesus.

Later the Christians called Saul by a new name. They called him Paul.

Paul became a great apostle. He told many people about Jesus.

Acts 9:1-19

Paul and Silas in Philippi

Sometimes Paul went far away to tell people about Jesus.

One time he sailed to the city of Philippi. His friend Silas went with him. They started to preach and teach about Jesus.

Some men in the city didn't like what they said. So they brought Paul and Silas to the rulers of the city.

The men told the rulers, "Paul and Silas are causing all kinds of trouble."

Other people came with the men. They also said bad things about Paul and Silas.

The rulers told soldiers to beat Paul and Silas with some sticks. Then the soldiers put Paul and Silas into jail.

The rulers told the jailer, "Lock the jail tight."

The jailer put Paul and Silas into a dark cell. He locked their feet in wooden blocks. Then he went to sleep.

Paul and Silas could not move their feet. And they hurt from being beaten. But they knew Jesus was with them.

Late that night Paul and Silas were awake. They prayed. They sang songs about Jesus.

Suddenly the earth shook. The doors of the jail flew open.

The jailer woke up. He saw the doors standing wide open. He thought all his prisoners had run away.

So he pulled out his sword.

He was going to kill himself.

Paul shouted, "Don't hurt yourself. We are all here. No one ran away."

The jailer picked up a light and ran into the jail. Then he led Paul and Silas out. He took them to his own house.

The jailer asked, "Sirs, what must I do to be saved?"

Paul and Silas answered, "Believe in Jesus and you will be saved."

Then Paul and Silas told the jailer and his family about Jesus.

They all believed the things Paul and Silas told them. They were baptized that same night. The house was filled with joy.

The jailer washed the cuts where Paul and Silas had been beaten. He brought food for them to eat.

The next morning the rulers came and talked to Paul and Silas. They told them they were sorry for putting them into jail. Then they let Paul and Silas go free.

That day Paul and Silas went to talk again with the Christians in Philippi. Later they went on to other cities and other lands.

Everywhere Paul and Silas went, they told people about Jesus the Savior.

Acts 16:11-40

What the First Christians Were Like

Many people became part of the Christian church on the first Pentecost.

God filled the first Christians with love and joy. They worked together to serve Him. They did whatever they could for Jesus. Others could see how much they loved Jesus.

Many Christians sold their land and houses. They brought the money to the apostles, and the apostles gave the money to those who needed it.

The first Christians still prayed at the temple in Jerusalem. But they also met in homes.

These Christians read God's Word and listened to the apostles preach. They prayed and sang together. They often shared their meals. And often they met together for the Lord's Supper.

Sometimes people tried to hurt the Christians. Then the Christians met in secret places.

Sometimes the Christians used a secret sign. They would draw a fish in the sand or on a wall. This drawing said to other Christians, "I believe in Jesus Christ, God's Son, the Savior." But other people saw only a fish.

The Christian church grew and grew. Soon the apostles needed helpers.

They told the Christians, "We want to spend all our time teaching, preaching, and praying.

Choose people to pass out food and money to those who need it. Be sure to choose people who are filled with the Holy Spirit."

So the Christians chose seven men to help the apostles.

The church kept growing. Groups of Christians lived in many different places. Each group chose someone to be their pastor.

The Christian church is still growing today. All believers in Jesus belong to His church.

We are all brothers and sisters in the family of God. God is our Father.

Even when we are selfish or jealous, God keeps on loving us. If we hurt one another, we can tell God we're sorry. We know He will forgive us for Jesus' sake.

He will also give us His Spirit so we may grow to be more loving and kind.

Also today, Jesus tells us, "Go to all the people in the whole world. Make them My disciples. Baptize them in the name of the Father, Son, and Holy Spirit. Teach them all about Me. And remember, I will always be with you."

Acts 2—6
Matthew 28:19-20